This is NOT it!

By Brett Green, M.A., L.M.F.T. -
Licensed Marriage & Family Therapist

BALBOA.
PRESS
A DIVISION OF HAY HOUSE

ISBN: 978-1-4525-5686-4 (sc)
ISBN: 978-1-4525-5687-1 (e)

Balboa Press books may be ordered through booksellers or by contacting:
Balboa Press
A Division of Hay House
1663 Liberty Drive
Bloomington, IN 47403
www.balboapress.com
1-(877) 407-4847

Because of the dynamic nature of the Internet, any web addresses or
links contained in this book may have changed since publication and
may no longer be valid. The views expressed in this work are solely those
of the author and do not necessarily reflect the views of the publisher,
and the publisher hereby disclaims any responsibility for them.

The author of this book does not dispense medical advice or prescribe the use
of any technique as a form of treatment for physical, emotional, or medical
problems without the advice of a physician, either directly or indirectly. The
intent of the author is only to offer information of a general nature to help
you in your quest for emotional and spiritual well-being. In the event you use
any of the information in this book for yourself, which is your constitutional
right, the author and the publisher assume no responsibility for your actions.

Any people depicted in stock imagery provided by Thinkstock are
models, and such images are being used for illustrative purposes only.
Certain stock imagery © Thinkstock.

Printed in the United States of America

Balboa Press rev. date: 11/27/2012

Dedication ~

I believe that simply the word "care" ... has little to no meaning without actions, faith and true intent. Actions and behaviors (not simply words) truly define and strip people to their core.

To my many supportive, wonderful family members and friends whose unconditional true actions, faith, love, and keen positive spirits have helped me to live over the years!

These loved ones continue to care and help me grieve, heal, and grow beyond boundaries! These people are angelic to me. Over the years, they have patiently supported my soul, rehabilitation, and movement toward a new and meaningful life ... at all times!

Even in the midst of my father's wage for his own life – he only cared for my own wellness versus his!

They have never doubted me as I have endured this incredible and (as yet) undefined journey! I love them beyond measurement, for all for eternity!

Epigraph ~

"Heart is the symbol of creative activity. Fire the heart with where you want to go and what you want to be. Get it fixed so deeply in your unconscious that you will not take no for an answer. To throw your heart over the bar means to throw your affirmation over every barrier, throw your visualization over your obstacles. In other words, throw the spiritual essence of yourself over the bar, and your material self will follow in the victory groove thus pioneered by your faith-inspired mind. Expect the best—not the worst—and you will attain your heart's desire"!

Thoughtfully Inspired by
Norman Vincent Peale

Contents

Foreword ~

Note from my mother

On a sunny afternoon in June of 2006, our world changed forever. After an especially severe asthma attack, a code blue hospital emergency signal was called on our son, Brett. We were told he was in a coma. Furthermore, we were told he would be later placed in a medically-induced coma in an attempt to stop the spasms his body was experiencing. He lived in this world every day, week after week. I'm not certain what day it was when he first tried to open his eyes. Although he couldn't keep his eyes open for more than a few seconds—and he was powerless to move any other part of his body—he was able to gently squeeze my hand when I asked him if he knew I was there. This was the start of an incredible journey for all of us—especially Brett.

Brett had been diagnosed with asthma when he was just six months old. Though the first two years of his life were filled with attacks that often landed him in an oxygen tent for various lengths of time, the frequency and severity of his attacks lessoned as he got older. In time, he was able to live a more active life. During his middle grades and high school years, he was exceptionally active. He had no problem participating in any and all forms of sports and activities that piqued his interest. He was on swim teams; played baseball, football, and basketball; ran track; skied; kayaked; hiked; and played golf (which he seemed to love the most).

He never allowed his asthma to stop him from doing what he loved to do. When he joined the army, he worried a bit about boot camp. I remember him sewing a pocket in his underwear for his asthma inhaler so he could always keep one with him. He never allowed anyone knowledge of his asthma or the severity of his attacks. I later learned he also buried an inhaler near his barracks and always kept one with him in his jacket.

Brett was told by so many doctors that "this was it", that there was little chance for improvement after his trauma. They told him that he would never walk again, but Brett chose the opposite path – the path of this is *not* it. For the past five years, Brett has handled his traumatic event well. With incredible determination, will power, positive thinking, acceptance, stamina, more determination, research, physical therapy, prayer (knowing that he can't conquer this mountain alone), and even more determination, he has triumphed.

I have an amazing son who has literally chosen to walk the walk: to offer himself in service to others. My son has not allowed his asthma and the subsequent paths in his life to make him a victim. He does not feel sorry for himself. He is a survivor!

It is Brett's fervent wish that this book can offer hope, knowledge, and insights to others during their own journey.

Patricia Patrick

Introduction ~

*Preliminary thoughts regarding
the Journey of my trauma*

Like anyone who has suffered such an unexpected traumatic event, I found my life dramatically changed forever!

I sometimes like to compare myself to a giant oak tree that has fallen unexpectedly. Hundreds upon hundreds of roots attached to that tree have become affected and altered. In my case, I felt as though I were that giant oak tree for many years, for so many people. I felt that there were so many roots that counted upon me to firmly rise up again as I have before. Even though countless people worked on this tree and tried until exhaustion to help, I could not rise! With me "fallen" and on center stage, people forgot that there were roots growing from and attached to this tree that were not acknowledged and rightfully cared for! For some, their deep wounds were not initially addressed—they were "merely" a *trauma witnesses* to the event and forgotten. I've heard the following many times: "You can't un-ring the bell!" Where there is one traumatic victim of a trauma—<u>let it not be forgotten</u>—there are many others entrenched, powerless and involved as well.

The journey to the before and after of my fall and rise has been a very long, painful, and arduous journey - It has also been a remarkable process to experience as I will try and capture within this book. I say *process* because it's an ever-continuing journey—one I doubt has a final destination. I know I am unable to pretend that I'm complete now. I'm unable to regain my previous life and just sit back and relax. On the contrary, it's a very harsh, knock-ya-back, humbling lesson that life is full of trials, tribulations, adversity, divine interventions, expectations, disappointments, improvements, and setbacks. Therefore, it's a daily process that requires living in the moment and using my own life-learned experiences to make it through each and every day. Even more importantly, it's a process I've come to know well and recognize (through my own lens) in others who have gone through traumas of a similar nature.

While traveling through this journey, I've learned a great deal about myself such as who I really am and what I'm capable of. I've learned from others as well! Each of us copes with trauma in an individual way. I've learned valuable insights from those who are processing personal traumas and yet, are striving daily for improvement within an incredibly tough mental, emotional, and physical battle. Some heal where improvement is indeed noticeable. I've also seen other survivors who have, in a sense, given up and the light is gone!

I've found that the trauma survivors who can move positively forward and heal best are those who can generally place themselves in the drivers' seat of their own life. With some significant mind control, they can look straight ahead in that great, big, directionless windshield called life! In that process, they can do their best to break away from fixating upon that smaller rear-view mirror of their life before that may often reflect their trauma or disability. That rear-view mirror of the past can be such an addiction, a temptation—it is often just easier than looking forward. Again, this can be so reflective of the traumatic event that may also keep one stuck in the past (and thus stuck in a great bed of hopelessness and lifeless mortality). In this case, there is no forward thinking … there is no forward movement. One need's to take just one second, one minute, one step, one moment… and make one difference at a time and always, always attempt to move forward.

I know how difficult it is to stop focusing on the before and after of a trauma (or the trauma of a loved one). The aftermath may be quite obvious physically (and visible to others) or simply known internally—emotionally or mentally. Like me, I imagine you can meander about mentally—looking and thinking at both edges of the road called life—and you can also emotionally, mentally, or physically crash. However, a main focus of this book is to offer the message that it's vital to stay mindful of your personal value, love existence, to remain grateful, and stay straight in the middle of your road of life. There is a life ahead for you to endure … but also one to experience and enjoy! If you can survive any intense trauma, it is my belief and message to you that you also can survive the aftermath as well. *Carpe Diem!*

In my particular traumatic event, I suffered a severe anoxic brain injury that later became known as post-anoxic action myoclonus (also known as Lance-Adams syndrome).

Initially, I did not record or journal my experiences routinely. I did not think that was the best avenue for me to release any current emotions regarding this experience. In the beginning, I was in complete *shock and denial*, and I thought I would just simply go home—that my life would return to normal! I didn't think I would need to review the event.

Later, as my condition persisted and worsened, the idea of expressing my experiences was brought up. I didn't think I would ever want to re-read those traumatic experiences and used that as a means of *justification and bargaining*. I used that excuse to avoid journaling (or being recorded, for that matter).

However, to this day, I have been powerless to stop thinking about those very experiences… day after day, everyday! In the end, I made the choice to write this book!

I have been trying to *accept* and write about these experiences and memories for the past several years and now I am doing just that.

I vividly remember thinking in the early stages of my trauma that having my picture taken was completely out of the question. I wanted to believe that I would heal whole, that I'd be home soon, and that my nightmare of nightmares would be over. I had no idea what the future held for me. No one who has not had the experience could know what is in store after a traumatic event. However, for myself and for others, I have taken time to learn. I now believe that pictures and journaling (or some positive form of expressing the trauma itself) may serve an incredible value for the survivor. I highly recommend this route. The reasoning, I believe, lies in the intent of each individual survivor, and it may actually serve a different therapeutic purpose for each one of us!

Trauma and subsequent disability are not something we ever plan for in our lives. Why would we? We plan for other things for our lives, such as college, marriage, careers, children, vacations, finances, and retirement. The unexpected world of trauma and disability is another world—a very shocking world. It is a world we don't know or recognize until we have to. It is a world we don't like to look at or think about until we have to. It is a world we don't know about until we are in it! It is a world the world avoids.

Some secondary emotions, such as *anger, fear, and grieving* are included in the trauma package. These are not unique. They are in fact quite normal, valid, and acceptable emotions to have. There are no correct reactions for one to display in response to a traumatic event. We all have our own untouched inner strength and means of handling life's curveballs.

I personally don't believe the grieving process can ever be complete. This is not to say healing cannot occur, but each person has his or her own individual path to follow toward acceptance. Again, it's a process! Grieving and mourning are ancient, natural rights. Thus, it is your right to feel and be heard within your own time and in your own way.

I now know—as I survive and adapt to the "second coming," the continuing rebirth of my new body—that I will be on this incredible journey forever. Prior to my trauma, I was a different person: a different man with a completely different "worldly" body—and therefore, held a very different identity! Certainly, as human beings, we all expect our lives to change over time for many reasons. Change can stem from shifts in income, family, work, or illness. Becoming a trauma survivor (or becoming disabled) is an area of human frailty we never allow ourselves to think about. As a relatively young and healthy man, at least I never did.

I thought that being a prior practitioner in the field of psychotherapy and mental health for many years made me sensitive to the needs of others. After all, I was in the field for sixteen years and I strived to help people. However, looking back, I believe I was sadly mistaken! I believe that so many therapists are blind to the real needs of the disabled and trauma survivor's! I look at how mistaken and misguided we as a society are when it comes to trauma survivors. As a society, we are generally not aware of the overall needs, tasks, and struggles that beset trauma survivors and the disabled. I have become even better at seeing and experiencing how others view those who are disabled—both professionally and personally. It is amazing to see the poor services, treatment, and acceptability nearly everywhere I go. *It is absolutely incredible, and will be forever indelible in my mind—I have had to sit on the other side of the couch.*

This is why I have chosen to walk the walk, to make the choice that "This is *not* it".

Cry as I might—and I've shed enough tears to fill an ocean—nothing will change my reality. I have simple human differences that are at times more visible and tangible, and my world as a trauma survivor is now comparable to having to live on a completely different planet than my birth planet.

From the time the sun shines and I open my eyes to the time the moon rises and my eyes close, I am challenged, I adapt, and I make it through yet another day. I do this with a fair amount of acceptance and happiness as do all survivors.

The work one must do during survival and healing post-trauma is unimaginable, but one purpose of this book is to help one reach a better understanding. For years, I wondered (and still do often) how do others make it, how do "they" get by on a daily basis. Specifically, how do others who have been through what I've been through choose to get by? How do people who are paralyzed manage their lives? How do people in wheelchairs (those in similar positions) get by? Do other people realize how hard it really is, or is it just me and other survivors? How do people who are far worse than I continue to endure the aftermath and keep smiling daily? How?

How one is and should be cared for, the validation of the grieving process, how one may heal, and tips for trauma survivors are all thoughts that will be addressed within this book.

This book will also offer an unforgettable glimpse into the world of the trauma survivor. It may provide those in need with a way to capture his or her purpose! Most importantly, my hope is to inspire people to find a way to document the journey should they find themselves or a loved one in the very unique world of trauma, grief, healing and ultimately, growth. It is an incredible and unforgettable ride!

It is also my hope that some think of this book as a way to begin to regain their own sense of normalcy—as well as their right to grieve and mourn the end of their old identity. This may ultimately serve as a stepping stone toward true healing. You have a right to move forward, one step at a time, and to heal … no matter what the circumstances!

Finally, I would like to mention that this journey isn't about numerous doctors and neurologists who may are mentioned throughout this book. It's not about the inappropriate things they said to one particular man—a man who lay helpless in a bed, strapped to a gurney, or bound to a wheelchair. It's not about that man being spoken to as if he were a child. It's not about a man who repeatedly heard the words, "This is it," as though his life were over.

This is about a man—myself, the trauma survivor—who is determined to survive: to talk, to walk, to endure, and to enjoy life! I want to experience this traumatic event and always say, "This is Not it," … I want to seize the day! This man wants to share his experience, his strength and his hope with his children—and with other victims of trauma!

Retrospective - One Year Later

Were the stars aligned differently? Was there a shadow cast upon the moon?

Or was it a sense of my own internal impending doom?

Looking back, what really happened on the evening of June 8, 2006?

I remember being so happy with my daughters all cuddled with me after dinner had been wonderfully fixed.

Although my breathing had become increasingly labored, I maintained minimal fear.

I had confidently learned to control my asthma for nearly forty-three years.

I called upon my brother for my own family insurance, and then I went to the hospital where I received immediate and critical care.

However, the longer I remained there, the more questions were posed and the more fears arose as I became acutely aware.

Once at the hospital, everyone appeared hurried. They all rushed around me, seemingly distracted and noncommittal.

I felt that I was the only one who knew that I was deathly ill!

As time elapsed and things went from bad to worse (and from worse to even worse)—"As critical as critical can get," said one doctor—my life became uncertain. I wondered, *Will I live or will I die?*

For me, time had evolved into slow motion, and my world became out of control. I kept asking, "Why me, why me, oh why?"

Everything seemed to spiral downward, and I distinctly remember hearing voices. There was fear and panic in the air, and someone said, "This is not good … he's not responding!"

I thought to myself, *how could this be? I just spent the past week golfing!*

For over eighteen days, my eyes remained closed!

I was medically sedated. My body did not twitch, move, or flex. And I was positioned in a frightening and deathly pose.

Family, friends, and loved ones all came to my bedside.

A constant and gentle aroma of love drifted in and out of my room, while whispers, prayers, and pleas were sent for me not to die.

Although hard to believe, somewhere, somehow, I heard and smelled them all. I felt every tug, hug, and kiss.

I silently cried deeper than deep inside, and I wished and wished and wished!

On June 26th, I awoke. My eyes briefly opened, and my nightmare turned confusingly real. Again, I felt death ... from my head to my toes. I could not move, speak, or feel.

Was I alive? Had I been in an accident? Was I paralyzed, never to move again, never to hug my children? Where was my faith?

What happened to me on June 8th?

Each night I felt empty and alone. I saw myself reflected on the mirrors above as I lay strapped, connected, and harnessed between lifesaving tubes, fluids, and machines.

All the while, my thoughts and memory were intact. I lay there thinking - this is not right, I'm a Green!

All the machines, treatments, nurses, therapists, doctors, nutritionists were striving to keep me alive.

Despite the mental, emotional, and physical challenges, consequences and questions—I often wondered ... should or would I survive?

Then it started. The uncontrollable body movements— earthquakes in my legs!

Indescribable, violent, uncontrollable, gut-wrenching shakes, jerks, and tremors that increased throughout my body each and every day.

They implied the answers to my condition lay within their medical degrees and books, and then they said I might be experiencing lasting side effects of the medical paralytics. Regardless, I was in everlasting and uncontrollable pain.

All I knew was that my mind, body, and spirit were completely and utterly drained!

Each day, I was engulfed in the clenches of despair, the grief that surrounded me, and my own internal fear.

I was beyond the point of heartache, past my emotional and physical breaking point. My eyes could no longer shed tears.

My body was exhausted. I was spent and thought there was nothing left. I was ready to give up. I was ready to die—I wanted to die! But I knew that I could not stop fighting for life.

Hearing my children's lovely poems and letters read to me—and then seeing their tear-soaked, bright, and innocent eyes.

And so I lived. I remained on life support machines and continued to receive critical care while staying cognitively in tune. I observed my family's desperate looks and saw their need for any lively signs from me.

But all the while, my body and mind were being poisoned and overdosed with a cocktail of drugs for all to see.

I couldn't speak, so I attempted to communicate to others by blinking my eyes using an alphabet board.

Despite the endless effort and kindness of my family and friends, however, it seemed that no one could understand me as I continued to pray to my lord!

I was helpless and hopeless. Doctors asked what I wanted and whether I was in pain.

But they always answered their own questions. Their answers were always in opposition to my own thoughts and feelings. I wanted to scream the opposite to them, but all in vain!

I asked at least a thousand times daily, *"Why did this have to happen"?" What did I do to deserve this"?*

The answer never came, and I continued to struggle— second by second, minute by minute, day by day, month by month—just to exist!

For fifty-one days, I visited what I know is hell. There was horrendous treatment and daily nightmares that somehow became real.

But through family perseverance and divine intervention, I was transferred to another hospital facility to hopefully get my mind, body, and spirit well.

I spent forty-six long, hard days in in-patient rehabilitation services. I was depressed, angry, and confused. I was unable to speak well or walk, and I so desperately wanted to see and be with my children.

But my family, friends, and the angels above were all there with me to help see that, in the end, my kids and I would be together again.

With nearly every goal unmet, I was discharged from rehabilitation services. At the time, I thought, *"I'm not ready; this isn't fair"*!

My coordination and balance were equivalent to a nine-month-old baby. I could not sit unaided, balance, walk, or talk well—and I was confined and strapped to a wheel chair!

What happened to me on June 8th, 2006? Well in short, I died from an asthma attack!

But with help from the angels above and the prayers from below, I was brought back!

However, as a result, I was ultimately diagnosed with post-anoxic action myoclonus… Lance-Adams syndrome.

I really didn't care what they had called it before or what they wanted to call it now. After all the months of medical guesses, speculation and treatment, all I wanted was to go home.

Although my journey was far from over, I left to heal and progress on familiar ground.

But what I experienced was an uninvited, tormenting, and raging emotional breakdown.

I went from being physically and mentally strong, athletic, confident, successful, and proudly independent,

to being completely, totally reliant and dependent!

Yet I worked harder than hard and struggled every day for improvement. I often pushed myself beyond my own limitations.

I desperately tried to regain lost weight and lost strength, and I tried to become independent again and create new expectations.

Although I was told that I improved each and every day.

I continued to experience emotional, physical, and mental exhaustion. I was completely dependent and struggled for the need and care that I had to receive every day … in every way!

Every day, I battled and felt alone.

Oh the sweat, the tears, the falls, the bruises, and the numerous broken bones.

After one year passed, my reality is that I am disabled. Maybe not forever—maybe? Although I still find myself looking back in life's rear view mirror, I also know I have to let go. No more asking, "What happened to me on June 8th?"

No more thinking, Was it God's plan, my fault, a matter of circumstance, or just plain fate?

As time passed, I thought, *"It is what it is" and I must focus on what to do next.* The answer came quickly for me, and I found it to be quite simple: to never, ever give up!

I believe without any doubt that I will survive, I will move forward, I will live and talk and walk again.

Make no mistake about it - I am determined to get my life back in the end!

So after all is said and done—and all the words have been spoken.

I find that this is a new day, a new month, a new year and a new man named Brett has awoken!

Brett Green (June 8, 2007)

A Personal Card to Me (June 8, 2007)

Although it's only been twelve months, there are times it feels like years. So many challenges, everyday a struggle and yes, so many tears.

But you did it, Brett—you remained strong. And certainly you've proven all the doctors wrong.

The fight you've had to wage has been daunting; every step along the way was a first. "I want my body back," "I want my life back" became your very thirst.

To breathe, to move, to sit, to swallow, to talk. And always in the back of your mind: "Will I ever be able to walk?"

A wheelchair allowed you to sit, a tracheotomy helped you to talk, and therapists helped you to stand. We all knew it was your courage, your determination, and of course, you were in God's hands!

There must have been times when you doubted, when the nights were too long. But with each dawn, you were able to choose a new and promising song.

You not only survived, Brett, you truly thrived.

And although the fight is not finished yet, I know you will walk again. I know you will get your life back…I'd bet my life on that!

With love,
Your Mother

Chapter 1: The Tree That Fell!

The first thing that I was aware of upon regaining consciousness was the knowledge that there were so many people hovering above and around me. Unknown voices spoke in desperate and urgent tones. There was the constant beeping and humming sounds of the multitude of machines. I could feel the many different handprints that pressed and lay upon me.

I was very aware of the strong and familiar odor of the hospital!

Although I had lost consciousness, I had not lost my cognitive awareness or acute senses. I was aware of and could hear, smell and feel what was going on around me, but I was unable to respond. At that time, I was in such a state of paralysis that I could not move one single muscle. The simple act of opening my eyes was beyond my reach. What had happened to me, I wondered desperately (yet in utter silence)? For a long time, I lay there motionless in the dark. And it was a long time before that question would be answered.

But I knew one thing was certain: from that moment on, life as I once knew it would never be the same!

As the story of my unique journey unfolds, I believe it is important to know who I was before my traumatic injury. I believe that this is a means to truly comprehend my many life changes and the new man that I would become. I often will say *traumatic injury* throughout this book. In my case, what I specifically experienced was a traumatic brain injury (TBI).

Prior to this event, my life was relatively normal. I am the youngest of five children and experienced a solid and positive early childhood and some very rocky and troubling teenage years. I'm fortunate to belong to a very large extended family with different branches of siblings, extended family members, friends, and acquaintances that I have made over the years. Some of these people became very *affected* and others became quite *infected* by my traumatic event. *Affected* and *infected* have quite different meanings to me. Those I consider who were affected were very troubled by my event, but were able to move forward and function within their lives. Those I consider who were *infected* were quite close to me and did not address their own wounds from my fall and some were not able to move forward with normalcy. This point will further be addressed in the chapter titled Grief: *A Normal and Priceless Process!*

As a child, I grew up as the classic "industrialist"—a boy who sold lemonade on the street corner, a boy who wasn't afraid to knock on doors to make friends. Further, I had no problems on any schoolyard making my way athletically. Though, occasionally, I also made some poor choices on those schoolyards. At any rate, I knew how to protect myself. I am told I could best be described as a very determined child who let nothing or no-one stand in his way.

I excelled in all sports while growing up. After creating my own trials in and then out of high school, I enlisted in the United States Army. There, I ran (or using military slang, *humped)* over six miles per day for what seemed like years. When I completed my commitment and was honorably discharged from the military, I had no problem reaching my goal of entering a university. In college, I earned a valued degree and cross-trained, secretly hoping to engage in professional sports one day given an opportunity. Regardless of the sport, I was a very active man prior to my traumatic event.

By standard measurements of success and happiness, my adult life was good. In fact, it was very good! If one were to ask me today what my definition was of a very good life, I would have a completely different response than what I may have said many years ago. I once took many things—even something as simple and commonplace as standing—for granted. Today, my definition of a good life would simply entail standing, balancing, or walking on my own. That's it! Perspective is really everything—perspective and acceptance of what life offers on a daily basis.

I had always tried to maintain strong physical health, and I believed in creating an environment of all-around self-wellness. A natural-born optimist and achiever, I was fit physically, emotionally, and mentally. I could barely contain my huge, active, and inner zest for life. I also set and maintained a high standard of life for myself. I believed in living life honorably and living in a way that would make my children proud of me. I believed in God. I served and boxed in the military, which I had always dreamed of doing as a child. I thoroughly enjoyed and committed myself to college, eventually earning a master's degree in counseling psychology. I married and raised three extraordinary daughters and a stepson I thought of as an extraordinary bonus to my life. In my younger years, I often worked two jobs to support and sustain my family. And they, in turn, sustained me. My children were the gasoline that always kept me going and made me complete. I always tried and thought of myself as a good man. I was comfortable in my skin. I felt like I was living the American dream.

Unfortunately and regrettably, in 2002, my wife and I divorced. I became a single father and the primary caregiver for my three wonderful girls who, at the time, were eleven, eight, and five. My stepson was seventeen at this time, and he continued to live with his mother. His living arrangement caused a lot of heartache for all of us because he was so loyal and consequently emotionally torn by the divorce. Over time, he has come to live with me throughout the years.

After the divorce, I suffered physically and emotionally (as people do when the dream of marital bliss ends). This is, by the way, a trauma in itself!

Despite the difficulty of the situation, I have always believed it isn't divorce or separation that necessarily causes conflict; *it is the resulting behavior of the parents that defines the tragedy for any children involved.* As a result, I worked much harder to provide financially for my children and ex-wife. Although my children have always been the single highest priority in my life, they became even more precious to me as a single father. I know now that I became a much better parent to my children after the divorce in many ways. My efforts at work began to pay off, and I began to make much larger amounts of money. Although I know parenting has no correlation to income—*parenting is all about love and presence*—I was fulfilling another part of my own American dream by becoming financially secure. Nevertheless, there is no job or amount of money that could keep my love or presence away from my children.

Moving forward to 2006, I decided to quit my position at the county superior court where I had worked as a family court mediator. I had been there for many years helping high-conflict parents resolve their child custody cases, parenting issues, or concerns. I made the choice to quit this position only eight days prior to my traumatic event!

It was a very intense position, and although I felt very confident in my abilities, I had become burned out by the predictably unpredictable long hours and days. I sometimes mediated cases late into the night. It was a job with no quitting time—there was always more work to do and to be done. I left for the day when the court calendar or cases were done for that day (generally after 5:00pm). However, I was unable to turn off my mind. Most of these cases occupied my mind for weeks or months—and some of the tragic cases even stayed with me for years.

As the primary parent to my three children and stepson, I decided that my court mediator position had become too difficult for both them and me. I spent two long days at court each week. Another full day was spent in my own private practice. Also, there were the one or two days spent writing very intense and powerful child custody evaluations—these demanded an extraordinary amount of time outside of the court, the office, and my home. It often required meeting with families and children and writing mentally exhausting and very thorough reports. It is extremely challenging to write a report that you know is going to change lives. These reports strongly influenced the court's decision and the lives of children. While in this position, I often felt like a kind of a court-hired guardian angel for these children and always tried to keep their best interests in the forefront!

I tried to keep this in mind as I worked case after case! I found myself working a job in which I often found myself mentally revisiting specific cases and the children involved while playing with my own kids, driving, watching TV, eating dinner, dating, etc. To say it was all-consuming and mentally draining would be putting it mildly.

I became mentally fatigued at the young age of forty-two and decided to become a professional golfer!

However, long before quitting my job, I had started my own private practice with the idea that my life was going to be spent golfing during the early morning, fitting in some clients during the middle of a few days, and heading home by 3:00 p.m. to be with my kids. I thought I could do this without any change to my income. I was ready for a major life change, and I was prepared to be the best father that I could be. My children have always been (and will always be) the core of who I am. They are my life and the reason for my existence. My children genuinely mean everything to me, and I truly believe I was placed on this Earth to parent each and every one of them.

My children are wonderful. They are strong, beautiful, mindful and spirited. However, on that day in 2006, they were all unprepared for the emotional upheaval they experienced. My stepson was twenty and living on his own, and my other three little girls were only aged fourteen, eleven, and eight. They are the main roots of this tree, and they experienced and suffered trauma in their own right alongside mine.

Try to imagine that enormous tree falling and the roots from that tree being ripped unexpectedly from the earth. This might be close to my children's perception of their world at that time. Their world was ripped apart in front of their eyes. Their trauma was, of course, different than mine (and from any adults who were close to my situation). I believe the trauma of my children should have been considered a part of—rather than being separate from—my trauma. My children experienced incredible, indescribable, heart-wrenching, and mind-altering pain as their tree was hauled away in front of their shattered eyes. It is painful and difficult for children and family members to accept trauma that befalls their loved ones. Everybody imagines that they have to be strong for the tree. What about the children?

As you can see, I still am an advocate for kids … especially my own! It is important to note that, nearly six years later, my children are still grieving, accepting, and more importantly, healing. They are dealing with the loss of their childhood or early adulthood and the father they once knew (and have had to get to know again). Any children associated with any trauma survivor should consider supportive counseling. Without professional assistance or support, their coping skills may not be adequate at this particular age or stage within their development.

I was told early in life—and this stuck with me—that my twenties were for learning. This was true for me. My college years were exceptional years; years only to be matched by the births of my daughters. I was told my thirties were for earning. This also turned out to be true. I climbed the ladder of success easily, and my family and I enjoyed the benefits of that success. My forties were going to be a decade for burning bright, and they certainly started out that way! My fifties were going to be a decade for yearning—the time for regrets: could have, should have, and would have's. Strangely enough, I couldn't remember what was supposed to happen in my sixties—or any decades beyond that. Perhaps it was because I worked so hard, but I never visualized that I would live that long. For some reason, I had it ingrained in my head sadly enough that I would die before my sixties.

Looking back, I did end my thirties burning bright. And I went into my forties with a large amount of optimism, despite my divorce. I had become very established in my career, and I earned enough income through my work to do most anything I wanted. My kids and I skied in the winter, hiked Yosemite in the spring, played on the beaches along the California coast in the summer, and vacationed in Lake Tahoe throughout the entire year. I was able to afford just about all that we ever wanted. I had recently bought myself several kayaks, and I was training with my brother for whitewater kayaking. I had also purchased a speedboat for family summer fun. You could certainly say we were burning bright during this time!

I have always yearned to be the perfect parent, but through this trauma, I have learned I can never be one—disabled or not. I had tried to provide my children with positive experiences, with opportunities and adventures for learning. Two months prior to my event, I was fortunate to be able to chaperone my eldest daughter's eighth grade class on a trip to Virginia and Washington, D.C.—places I've always wanted to visit. I had planned on providing and enjoying the same experience with each of my two younger daughters. But, due to my physical limitations, it was and is now impossible to do so. I am grateful to have had the experience once (with my eldest). Although my two younger daughters have been fortunate to be allowed on this special trip, it's me that is left behind now. I'm unable to chaperone and protect them, as had been promised to each of them years earlier.

Despite my eternal optimism and quest for improvement, sometimes it is difficult to come to the realization that many of the memories in my mind (and all of the photographs that surround me) are now in the past, never to be seen or experienced again. This is a profound realization! I mention this because so many of these activities have become a memory or a picture on the wall, and this serves as a reminder of what used to be. That needs to change. I now have pictures of myself atop a mountain that I may never climb again next to photographs of myself in a wheelchair on a beach. It is so important to remember that it is still me pictured in both photos.

I believe it is of vital importance for trauma survivors to never give up and to find what they can do in the aftermath. Hang new pictures and create new memories to put in place alongside the old ones for all to see. Let me assure you that, through daily efforts, strong and positive affirmations—and through the passage of time—finding a new person and identity from within is indeed possible!

Chapter 2: What Happened?

What happened to me that night (and how the events unfolded) is still somewhat unclear and puzzling to me. I was born and have lived with asthma my entire life. Thus, I had experienced many attacks prior to that attack. I had been hospitalized too many times to count throughout my lifetime, but it had never held me back. I had always thought I was in control of my condition, and I was convinced that I always could be.

Early in life, I learned to control my asthma with a quick use of a "fast acting" inhaler. For the rare severe or emergency situation, I'd use an in-home nebulizer. However, on the evening of June 8th, 2006, nothing worked. For some unknown reason, that particular attack seemed different to me.

Yet my denial was still firmly in place, and my internal red flags still didn't flare up enough for me to call for help. With my children surrounding me in fear, I was still trying to remain in control of the situation. But my inhaler spray and the nebulizer were having no effect, which was very unusual. I became increasingly anxious, which ultimately led to a full-blown, frightening asthmatic attack. My thoughts began to race out of control regarding my options at the time and the potential consequences. Meanwhile, I was still trying to maintain complete composure for the security of my children's eyes.

I was still battling for air with my nose and mouth. Even though they were in my front pocket, I was unable to locate my car keys. I realized that I would not be able to drive myself to the hospital on my own as I was initially thinking. That led to increasing fear, panic, and frustration. At that time, not only did I realize that I was unable to inhale, but I began to notice that I was not able to exhale either. I was so scared—deathly scared—but I was still trying to remain calm. It was becoming increasingly difficult to try to figure out what to do next. All I could think to do was to pray for a miracle! I had no choice but to sit down as I became increasingly exhausted.

On her own my middle daughter called my brother, who lived very close by to come right away and help me. She had asked me earlier if she should call 911, and I had calmly told her not to. I didn't want her to be afraid. I still thought that I had everything in control at that time.

It was my decision—one that turned out to be a very wrong decision, and one that led to unforeseeable consequences. The decision not only affected me, but especially my daughter, who would be haunted and infected by those choices for years. At that time in that moment of crisis, I was incapable of thinking of my roots. In her case, she has carried a sense of guilt that if she had only called 911 earlier (and followed her own instincts); her daddy would be "okay today." As I stated earlier, children handle situations such as grief and trauma differently. From my experience, I believe that after my initial trauma, they should have been more a part of my experience than kept apart from it. I must add that I also believe children should be supported in some form of expressive therapy or form of counseling following a trauma event.

After taking one look and quickly assessing my condition, my brother knew that he had to call for emergency medical assistance immediately. Although I still believed that I could make it to the hospital solely with his help, I was also aware that I was literally fighting for each breath, each step and each minute. I was struggling to stand upright. I clearly remember all the horrific and fluid thoughts of my own mortality that floated in and out of my mind during that time.

Had my daughter not called my brother at that second, and had my brother not known to call for an ambulance at that very moment, I know now that my worst nightmare would have come true: I would have died at home in front of my all my children.

It is truly difficult to articulate what it feels like to be in the grips of an acute asthma attack or to be in complete asthmatic mode. There is nothing that can compare with the reality of an asthma attack. There is literally no air coming into our going out of your body (including your brain and central nervous system). It is nearly impossible to explain the confusion of thoughts and feelings that cause one to ask questions such as, "Can I have just one more breath?" or "Am I going to die?" Try to imagine, just for a moment, that you're in a tub of water and your head is being forcibly held under water until you struggle for breath. Just before you inhale water, your head is pulled back out for a quick gasp of air before being shoved back under. If, against your will, you repeat this process a thousand times, you might be able to comprehend somewhat what I went through while enduring this severe asthma attack.

Despite my situation, I remember not wanting to draw any attention from my neighbors. I told my brother (when he called 911) to tell the operator to send only an ambulance— no fire trucks or police. Near death, I was still cognizant enough to feel embarrassment about something I had no control over. It is funny to think about it now, but at the time, I was very serious about this. In any case, within what seemed like an instant, I heard what sounded like the entire city's SWAT team, police force, fire department and ambulance fleet. They were all coming to my home, and ultimately, to my life's rescue.

I remember being concerned about the number of people that were in my home. There were so many voices and feet rushing about, and I couldn't discern what was being said about me. The emergency teams there immediately gave me high doses of oxygen, placed me on a gurney, and quickly rushed me outside my home and into an ambulance.

Through all of this confusion, my thoughts kept returning to my kids. And there they were, watching the horrific scene of their father dying before them. Before being taken away, I remember being wheeled out and fighting to offer words of reassurance to my children. I gave them all a "family thumbs up sign" because I expected to be home shortly. Unfortunately, my initial hopes did not come true.

I will never forget looking into the fear within my children's tear-soaked eyes as I was whisked away amidst all the noise, fear, strangers, and chaos. Sirens were blasting down the street. My children were left standing on my lawn in the dark night ... alone!

What I had initially hoped for and what came to be my reality are not the same. I will forever wonder what the answer to the following question is: what really happened on the evening of June 8th, 2006?

I live less than two miles from the hospital where I received initial treatment. The ambulance ride seemed to whisk by in seconds. Once they had me settled in a bed in the ICU department at the hospital, I remember thinking that things were taking way too long—I still couldn't breathe! Though exhausted, in between a few gasps of air, I was blurting out commands and orders to doctors and other medical staff to give me adrenaline and epinephrine—and to *hurry*! However, it seemed that the staff in that room only gave me quick glances. They did not listen to my advice that I had learned from past successful methods of treatment. They seemed either too hurried or indifferent to listen further to what I was trying to communicate. They then walked away from me and seemingly decided that they had done all they could. At that moment, my fear became intense, and my reality more fearful—like never before in my lifetime.

Before, my fear with asthma was, to a great extent, defined as a short pause in life in which I experienced some trepidation, but knew that within a few minutes, the medicine would kick in. I knew I'd be fine, and the fear would leave and be replaced by a sense of control. Life would resume.

In fact, looking back on my life, I had always thought that I had been in control of everything, each aspect. This was the first time I was in a state of such complete fear that I allowed myself to believe that I might be at the end of my life, that I was going to die. And death meant leaving my children unprotected and unprepared—along with every other horrific thing I had ever imagined. For some unknown reason, I also remember lying there thinking that I had predicted from a very young age that my death would somehow be asthma related. This is, perhaps, because I have so many early memories of being in an oxygen bubble or tent (in my infancy and early childhood years). Those episodes have been forever etched into my psyche. I don't know why it was, but there I was with the same thoughts I had carried for nearly forty years. Maybe this was it?

As my fear and impatience seemed to take my last bit of air, I finally remember hearing the most welcoming words spoken by what seemed to me the most beautiful and calm voice: "He's beginning to stabilize." The doctors and staff had been giving me a multitude of shots and treatments that had appeared to help me gain control of the ability to breathe on my own. That helped me regain a sense of calm and comfort. I was surrounded once again and brought to that sense of familiarity—once again, I was overcoming the difficult symptoms of an acute asthma attack. I believed all was well!

Chapter 3: Hospital I—Can I Just Go Home?

I endured my shortest stay at this first hospital. My memories of this stay are more sparse, and some are even more dreamlike. I do remember that my brother immediately came to visit me after checking on my children. I remember asking him to go back and stay at my house for the rest of the night to comfort my girls and reassure them I would be okay. I also remember remaining in the ICU ward under close supervision and finally stabilizing into a calmer state after what seemed like a very long time.

Ultimately, I was transferred (for rest and sleep) into the pediatric ward due to room space. Into that next morning, I rested and the doctors and I felt I was ready to go home. There was even talk of my discharge that afternoon! However, I remember just prior to being discharged— but before I was able to actually sign myself out of the hospital and go home—one doctor expressed unusually high concern. She requested that I attempt to complete a trial run. This was a simple request to walk to the elevator door and back. I remember thinking that the request was absurd. I just wanted to get it over with and get home. *Of course I can do this I thought...* I began to walk forward with confidence. As I began my trek down the hall, the doors of the elevator seemed to get further and further away and become smaller and smaller in size. When I finally reached the elevator door and turned around, I realized that, once again, I was unable to inhale. At that point, getting back to my starting point seemed impossible. It was then and there, that I experienced another major asthmatic attack. That was it! A single moment in time changed my life forever. That was the beginning of my new life—a new transformation, a new beginning, a new body, a new man, a new life, and a new world! When I refer to the word "new" here, I cannot understate the meaning of this word and use it strongly as a reflection of a "change" to my life.

My next memories are very vivid and real, yet somehow very vague. There are an assortment of wild pictures etched forever into my brain of the hospital staff tugging and pulling at me, shouting my name, and saying, "This is not good. He's not responding!"

I was able to read over the hospital notes at a later time, and it appears that, at that moment, I "coded" in front of the elevator doors. All my major organs began to shut down. The transcripts read as follows: "He's purple from nipples to head." They later say: "Stomach to head." I gasped that I had an actual heart attack during this time and went into a coma. This was it ... if not for the extraordinary, coordinated efforts of all of the doctors who brought me back to life. This seems impossible to me now as well as incredible. Yet there it is in print!

Tears fill my eyes as I relive that experience, that resurrection. I've had to willingly adapt and accept my new abilities and disabilities each waking day. I believe all trauma survivors have to relive their "rebirth" as a measure of working toward acceptance.

I learned later that I was placed on paralytics for an extended time as part of my medical treatment. I lay flat and totally motionless on my back in a coma state for nearly three weeks. My body never moved; there was no twitch or flex. For all intent and purposes, during this period, I was dead. Yet I was medically kept alive by high doses of oxygen, a respirator, a ventilator, and a vast array of medical technology. I was harnessed to an assortment of graphic machines that illustrated every possible function of my body. My mother told me later that she had counted over fifteen fluid bags or IV tubes connected to me.

Throughout those three weeks, my family was in what I call <u>traumatic confusion</u>; *that is, I believe they had no certainty as to whether I would live or die. They were still in a state of complete shock and denial in terms of coping with my situation.*

My home became a rotating resting ground for family members and friends. There were nearly forty messages placed on my answering machine from the hospital staff during the brief period of my stay. These messages mainly requested my family to urgently get to the hospital because my condition was uncertain or becoming worse. These messages were unbelievable to hear once I was finally was able to return to my home—it was almost surreal to hear of my own impending death.

I don't remember a certain white light or hands reaching out to me as I often hear described when talking to other people's reflections on near-death experiences. I have heard of so many different experiences that I suspect that this experience might be unique to the individual. What I do remember for myself is being completely aware yet in a form of sleep day after day. I remember wanting (and trying desperately) to wake up, but being unable to do so. I just couldn't!

I couldn't see anything, but black reflections or black dots as I tried to view my surroundings. I could hear people musing around me and feel their touch upon my body. I remember that, the harder I tried to open my eyes and awaken the more tired and frustrated I would become. Eventually, I would fall into a deeper sleep within my sleep. Make no mistake, I do remember hearing the voices of medical staff, my family members, and my friends— especially the voices and cries of my children! On occasion, my mother would talk to me very close to my face. I could actually smell her. She would often squeeze my hand to let me know she was there. And I did know -- I just couldn't tell her! One special friend would sit by my bed for hours, day after day, talking to me, recounting memories, and touching me. I also remember hearing the words from a long past loved one upon seeing me stated, "What have they done to you?" It was amazing to talk to those people later. I had remembered exact statements, moments and had clear visions of them in my room. It was as if I were looking at a scene shot from above me at times—and it was being played out as I lay there.

Regardless of what you may read or hear from others, medical staff and the like - you should never give up on talking to those who are in a coma, have a brain injury, or are unconscious. They may be able to hear you loud and clear, and they need your voice for emotional and mental security. They need your voice to provide them with a sense of hope! Medical staff should know they are being heard. I know this is true not only for me, but also for many other cases like mine.

I believe I opened my eyes for the first time on June 24th—but only for a very brief moment. I immediately recognized my mother, but I couldn't move or keep my eyes open. They would shut only seconds after opening them. I don't think I had the strength to keep them open at that time. However, this would happen occasionally and give my family tremendous hope and joy. I could sense this from the noise and jubilation I heard from the people present in and out of my room. I regained what I would refer to as a light consciousness sometime in late June. As time progressed, I heard more and more, and I was able to stay awake for longer and longer periods.

I have come to refer to this as my awakening after death party. I gradually became more aware of my surroundings: my many family members, friends, and supporters who came to visit. At one point, I was able to awaken fully, and I was more alert than usual. I first remember seeing my Aunt Helen and my Uncle Dave. They appeared to be in a state of panic over my situation or condition. I could not understand their apparent looks because I still somehow thought that all would be well soon. I hadn't realized how much time had passed.

Then I remember recognizing all of my loved ones, especially my children. I remember their joyous tugs and hugs. There is nothing better to awaken to the love and gratitude of one's own children. Along with them were my mother, my sister, my brother Craig, and (off in the corner) my stepson and father. Many others gently came in and out of my room, filling the space with a gentle aroma and sense of love, kindness, and compassion. Although, due to my condition, I still couldn't understand all of what was being said or asked of me. I knew that they were looking at me puzzled. More importantly, I was looking back at them with determination, and they knew this. I was still in a very dreamlike state, yet I was cognitively aware to a certain extent as well.

I will forever remember the sounds of the background machines and my awareness of my new limitations of movement. I had no range of movement at all! I did not have complete control of my eyelids, and I could not feel where my arms and legs were. At that point, I couldn't remember that it was an asthma-related issue, and I imagined that I must have been paralyzed in a car accident (or something possibly worse). My memory was blank! I wasn't able to get answers as far as what had happened—both because I couldn't speak and because nobody offered explanations. It was apparently assumed that I remembered why I was there or that the event was considered to be too traumatic for me to deal with at that time. In any case, I asked myself over and over again: *Why am I in the hospital? Why am I here? What is the matter with me?*

Although my family felt the treatment and medical staff were second to none at the first hospital, my primary insurance carrier deemed me to be stable after a relatively short period. Against the wishes of the initial hospital's direct staff and my family, I was forcibly transferred to the primary hospital of my insurance carrier. I don't remember any of the medical personnel that ultimately saved my life, and I regret that. But it's a small world. I do remember being wheeled out on a hospital bed for transfer and seeing a nurse that I had provided professional work for previously at Family Court Mediation Services. Unfortunately, I remembered the ruling hadn't gone in her favor in spite of my hard work. I thought briefly about what I did or didn't do for her case and about the turn of events. In any case, as I was hurried out, she stopped and was kind to me upon my discharge. We exchanged greetings simply with our eyes. I felt a sense of compassion from her.

Until I went deep into the trenches and did battle with them myself, I never understood the bureaucratic mess that exists within insurance companies and the United States health care system.

I had over fifteen tubes of some sort attached to me (such as a ventilator, nose tubes, and countless IV tubes), and I was still in an induced semi coma state. When I was ultimately ordered to be transferred, my family asked one doctor how critical I was. The doctor quickly said that I was "As critical as critical can get."

Chapter 4: Hospital II—
I'm Going to Die!

I knew upon arriving at the new hospital that things would be different. It felt like I was on a new planet. There seemed to be no knowledge of what I had been through, my condition, or my state. There was an immediate discussion with regard to the removal of my ventilator. I remember this vividly. I could hear a respiratory therapist (RT) being told to remove my intubation and this filled me with fear because it was my mental life line. I had no control of my body, and I was at the complete mercy of the medical staff surrounding me. (What a new meaning *mercy* has for me now!) I was so completely helpless. Once the intubation and ventilation tubes were removed, I was pushed upright on my hospital bed. A very unique oxygen mask was then placed over my face. I will never forget the indelible smell of the pure air that I breathed in. I could see the medical team looking at me. My mother and brother were also there, attempting to help me in this treatment. However, their mere presence and repeated nervous chants to calm me down and "breathe" only increased my agitation. I know that the core of this fear and agitation was that the new treatment was not working and my overall health was not improving. I could see the doctors shaking their heads in the negative fashion, some with their mouths wide open.

I was struck by the look of horror on my mother's face. She appeared so sad, helpless, and hopeless, yet she continued to verbally order me to fight on! Her face looked as though she had not slept for days, yet she was speaking in the tone of a drill sergeant. I always knew I had a very strong mother, and having gone through this ordeal, I believe there is no one stronger in terms of perseverance, positive determination, love, and flat-out mothering than mine. I felt her love and strength push me through this trauma (as I still feel to this day)!

I distinctly remember the moment that would change my life forever. A tremendous convulsion began moving throughout my body. It started in my feet, moved to my legs and arms, and then it took complete control. It reminded me of a volcanic eruption within my own body. My entire body was shaking violently, and I felt like I was on fire. I had absolutely no control over my body, and I was unable to talk. Physically, I was in complete distress; my system was overworked, my muscles pulled and flexed as I fought a battle with life for air. There was a constant stream of sweat that poured out of my body by the minute, so I was unable to stay hydrated. The more I tried to focus and concentrate on stopping the shaking, the worse it got.

My legs continued to shake violently. Through my previous work and education, I knew emotional management techniques, meditation, mindfulness, relaxation, and many other skills that helped with anxiety and stress reduction. I knew several positive breathing techniques and had a great sense of cognitive control, but at that moment I was in too deep a state of distress and fear. Nothing seemed to work.

Because I was nearly bouncing off the bed, one of the doctors in charge at the time walked up close to my bed and actually asked me if I was making the movements and "shaking on purpose". My knees were coming closer and closer to hitting my head as he spoke, and I couldn't believe I was being asked such a question. My body was beginning to contort more and more. I remember a young female intern fearfully and tearfully looking from the distance as my symptoms and pain increased. With each shake and quake, it felt as though the bones in my feet, ankles, legs, arms, shoulders, and abdomen were breaking and tearing. I was in an ever-increasing state of shock with increasing panic and fear. I wanted to reach out to the doctor for asking such a question, but of course, I couldn't. Physically, I had absolutely no control. I was at his complete mercy. I could only shake my head no in response which seemed to bring on further and more distressing tremors and convulsions. My body went into such a crazed state that all parts started to contort more before all others present.

As I stated earlier, I learned that this was only the beginning of my real understanding of the word *mercy*. Being at the mercy of the medical staff at many hospitals, I have to take the opportunity to say that though some staff were wonderful, compassionate, and caring in their work and fields, however, there were far too many who appeared to be indifferent and careless in terms of their work and patients. In my case, I felt that I was just another trauma patient. Nobody knew me. I wasn't anybody's son or brother. I wasn't a relative. I wasn't famous. I was just another patient who had been expected to die. And as such, I was treated like I was dead already!

During this period, my body was in an extreme state of life that I call *fight mode.* I tried resisting each convulsion and shake. I continued to drip sweat like I was in a steam room. The monitors attached to me that indicated such things as blood pressure, pulse, heart rate, oxygen retention, etc. were all off the charts. I was asked again by another doctor if I was doing all of the shaking and convulsing on purpose! My symptoms were as unknown to this hospital and staff as they were to me. However, I still had no idea why I was in a hospital nearly a month after admission, and the doctors still had no idea how best to treat a patient with my symptoms.

I have experienced the chills before, when my body couldn't stop shivering no matter how many blankets I used or who I snuggled up to. However, what I was experiencing were body chills and shaking beyond what I've ever seen, experienced, or thought physically possible. They seemed demonic and on the volume of a possession within. I felt as though my head was on fire, my heart had stopped, my kidneys exploded, my liver was riding some kind of merry-go-round, and my ability to draw air into my lungs had simply disappeared.

I had never felt more helpless and powerless in my life, but somehow I managed to mouth out the words "*help me*" to a respiratory therapist (RT) standing near me. At the time, the RT was being told by the doctor in charge to re-ventilate me immediately by placing what looked like a small, red horseshoe being placed upside down to the back of my throat. I also remember being injected with a tranquilizer called Ativan. This was the nurses' favorite drug for me. I later learned that for every pain or onset shake or tremor I experienced, some medical staff person said, "Get the Ativan." This was often combined with a morphine drip or some other brew daily. My quality of life was diminishing at this hospital, and I knew I would be at the continued mercy of the medical staff.

By this stage, still no one had bothered to tell me what was happening or what had happened to me! I still had no idea of what was causing my symptoms, and I was left to ponder, wonder and guess. I had never seen or heard of anything like my condition. Nobody seemed to know why the shaking and paralysis was happening, and more importantly, how to treat these symptoms. The only solutions offered entailed putting me to sleep or injecting me with cocktails of multiple drugs. All I thought at the time was that I was becoming an experimental patient for this particular medical team due to the staff's inability to recognize my condition or treat me adequately. Thus, I believed I received what I refer to as guesswork treatment due to their lack of knowledge. It appeared they were as powerless as I was. I was thinking where's the character from "House" on a popular television show -- I really needed him!

During my stay, I became somewhat dependent on the multitude of drug potions and combinations. These were rushed to me by frightened staff at every shake, tremor, or attempt I made to move or talk. It began to be too much, too painful and difficult for staff and others to watch me at times. I remember there was an Independence Day celebration on July 3rd, 2006 in the ICU ward. Watching a nurse light sparklers at the balcony or windows of my room, I immediately thought of my children and celebrations past. I began to shake with a heavy heart and emotion shortly afterward. I remember her saying to me as she injected me with Ativan and another drug that she just couldn't bear watching me in any more pain. There are too many times during my stay when the unfortunate medical staff was as fearful and bewildered as I was. I truly have learned that there is nothing worse to fear than fear itself … or of the unknown!

They had no idea what the best course of treatment was for me, and I was left unknown and alone to contemplate my fate.

An early memory I have from my stay at that hospital was being positioned for the first time in a way that enabled me to see my toes. The nurse first lifted my head, and when she pulled her hand away, my head collapsed back on the pillow. There was a sad exhale in the room that seemed to echo off of the walls I remember. My body was experiencing such severe atrophy that my neck couldn't even hold up my head. I was unable to lift my head, arms, or legs at all on my own. I couldn't believe it. I tried over and over for what seemed… forever!

At that time, I indicated a strong wish to see my hands, feet and toes. A whirlwind rush of thoughts of Brad (my brother) immediately came to mind after finally being propped up in such a way to do so.

My brother Brad had died on November 18, 2001, and he had been hospitalized prior to his death. Unable to move, my mind spun out of control with notions of my own certain impending death. My body was falling apart in front of my own eyes. I could not lift any self body part. I had hand-hang and foot-hang terribly; the muscles in my hands and feet were deteriorating to such an extent that keeping them upright was incredibly painful and impossible without assistance. Upon seeing my hands, fingernails, feet, and toes ... they looked exactly like my brother's did just prior to his death. It was at that time that I was sure I was going to die!

There was one nurse who took extraordinary care of me— despite the distress of my existence at the second hospital. From the first time we met, I knew immediately that I could trust her and that I was safe with her. I tried to request her nightly because she worked the swing/graveyard shift. I cannot say enough about what an incredible person this nurse is, how much extra attention she paid to my well-being and safety. I will always love her deeply for her "care". She even bought me shoes on her own to help prevent further foot-hang. As she became aware of my fears and growing concerns, this very special nurse often worked extra hours to ensure my safety and see that my needs were being met. This wonderful lady proved that there were members of the hospital staff who still cared about my quality of life—and whether I lived or died. For me, the nurse was a god send. Without her there at times, I would have died. I do know this to be true!

There were days, unfortunately, when this particular nurse had the night or day off. I was always trying to understand what happened to me. I was never able to receive any answers regarding my own history, current needs, or limitations of my body. I kept thinking and believing at all times that I would eventually be fine and sent home. When my favorite nurse wasn't working, this proved to be a battle on top of the battle I already faced as a trauma patient.

Despite all of the technology and machines that I was attached to, I also needed to have a tracheotomy within my throat to help sustain my life. This turned out to be a painful process for me and having to be repeatedly suctioned in the throat and mouth on an hourly schedule was excruciating. Different RT's would uncap my tracheotomy and suction the mucus in and around my throat and airways. I had so many different respiratory therapists. They all seemed to have their own way of doing things. They told me how things should be done, and each had an opinion about the efficacy of others' work. As is true with any job in life, some RT's were more skilled than others, and some took pride in their work. However, it seemed that, during the course of my stay at this hospital, I generally had indifferent professionals who displayed an utter lack of concern regarding any pain being inflicted. It was not unusual for an RT to go too far down my throat and painfully scratch my vocal chords. They were seemingly robotic regarding their work, and they displayed little concern about side effects to the patient as they suctioned.

From my experience, one's outside perceptions of being cared for at a hospital are not necessarily accurate. It is an absolutely crazed state of existence when you *know* that each day may be your last. It's recognition of true human powerlessness. Though the outside world sees **Urgent Care** in big, bold letters painted on any hospital, that may not always be true. In my case, I would scream without sound. I had no voluntary movement, and I lay within a coffin of despair each second of everyday. I found no urgency in getting me adequate care.

There were too many life-threatening events during my stay at the hospital to try to describe. If it were not for the grace of God, I'm pretty certain I would have died. One such incident stands out in my memory: the alarms went off on my life-support machine because I was choking on my own vomit. I had begun to regurgitate my fluids from my nose tube, and I knew that precious seconds was ticking away. Within time, I believed either nobody was within hearing distance, or nobody bothered to get up. I was in a state of terror as I watched my vomit run down my air tubes and into my airways. My airways were, once again, becoming restricted. The alarms on my bedside seemed to last forever, and I took what I thought was going to be my last breath. However, by unexpected chance, a nurse from a different unit happened to walk by my room during that very fine timeline between life and death. That nurse saved my life. I somehow remained conscious during this nightmare and was suctioned. This male nurse then got the attention of my regular nurse (who seemed shocked and annoyed that something could happen on her rounds despite the sounding alarms). The nurse that saved me left believing that I was in good hands. Caring, professional, compassionate hands. However, unfortunately, that was not the case.

My regular nurse was one of the many professionals who I referred to as terrorist nurses. They exert power and control over their patients rather than compassion and care. There were times that I cried when I found out which nurses were to be assigned to me. I knew they would show a complete lack of concern for my well-being and quality of life. I was certain that any day with them could potentially be my last. On any given shift, I was never sure what type of care I would receive from these people—or if I would actually receive the care.

A nurse is defined by the Merriam-Webster Dictionary as one who cares for the sick and infirm. The key word is *care*.

The nurses definitely appeared stressed by my around-the-clock need for critical care. That in itself seems oxymoronical—my entire stay was in the ICU. They shared and showed their frustration with me often by yelling while doing routine aspects of their jobs or by being extremely rough. Examples of this rough behavior cropped up often when they had to change my sheets or hospital gowns. I remember one nurse and RT calling it a buck-a-roo when a patient was moved from one nurse's care to another's. Due to my special needs, I found myself described in that way often by the nurses as they reported in and out for their shifts. I found the reference very dehumanizing.

There were days I pushed the alarm button or accidentally hit it with my hand and discovered that a nurse would not respond regardless of my situation. There were also other times when I would be choking on mucus, and it would not be suctioned until right before a staff member noticed me about to pass out.

However, the times that my family or friends were around were always much better. The specialists, therapists and nurses gave me much better attention and visibly took care of my room and overall needs. They completed their rounds on time and ensured that all appeared (and was) well. I found this to be despicable and interesting at the same time, but I was unable to communicate the difference of care coherently to any family member or friend. I was always reluctant to have my family leave, and more often than not, I had them stay until late into the night with me. Being alone left me vulnerable.

I was confused by the weekly rotation of the doctors and specialists during the months that I stayed at the second hospital. The lack of social and cultural competence they possessed as they shifted by each bedside was appalling. No doctor seemed to have a mind of his or her own; they all seemed incapable of thinking for themselves. It appeared that all the doctors looked at my particular chart for no more than a few seconds before following what the previous doctor had recommended. This was without assessing for themselves whether or not I was improving or not. There was nobody looking further into my condition—or the success or failure of my medication and treatment.

The doctor who I initially saw treated me like I was an infant who was unable to understand. Knowing I couldn't communicate with him, he would ask and then reply to his own questions … for me. I was on fire inside each time he did so. He was incredibly self-indulgent and unable to treat me like an equal adult male. Unfortunately, I found that every doctor I encountered was equally reluctant to make a definite assessment regarding my treatment—or to speak to me rather than at me or about me.

My frustration increased due to my inability to move and speak, so my family brainstormed and created an alphabet board that would allow me to communicate. Initially, I would simply blink at letters they pointed to and spell out words to ask or answer questions. To my recollection, the first question I asked was whether I was going to die. My sister quickly replied with tears, "No, Brett, you've already survived!" With this tool, I was also able to begin a sort of dialogue with the medical staff. I finally gained a further understanding of their assessment of my current functioning (as measured by their multitude of tests). Most importantly, I was able to gain a deeper understanding of my brain injury that was caused by an asthma attack. I finally learned what actually happened! I immediately flashed back on the many days, weeks and months that had passed by, and asked where all of my kids were. I needed my roots! Within my mind, I also flashed back upon the trauma event and my road to here.

However, somehow I was unable to believe that asthma was the main trigger or issue at hand. I still wondered what really happened on June 8, 2006!

I knew very little about the extent of my injury aside from the anoxic brain trauma resulting from my asthma attack that I was told. I was also told very little regarding a prognosis, but I soon began to surprise everyone with my ability to communicate and account for events. My memory prior to and throughout the journey seemed to shock the many doctors and specialists involved—and it provided my family with much needed relief. Although my family was relieved, I knew something was still very wrong with me because I was paralyzed, and felt gravely ill within! I still could not understand how it all came from an asthma attack. I was very suspicious. I was cautious of everyone who came in contact with me. I felt that I was in a very unsafe and dangerous environment and begged "everyone" repeatedly to be taken home. As I've said before, I truly felt as though each day was going to be my last.

Being sedated and on my back for so long, it didn't take long for my body to be eaten away. I believe I lost over forty pounds in a little over a month, and I was much too weak to lift almost any part of my body on my own. Although I shook violently when I moved or when my emotions (such as anger, sadness, and fear) began to surface, I could lie still for long periods of time without any tremors. However, if I began shaking in one leg, it generally afflicted the other leg … and then made its way to my abdominals and swept through the rest of my body. I felt I was constantly fighting for survival as I attempted to resist each convulsion, shake, and tremor with all my might every waking day!

I learned to lie on my back and prop up my arms and legs with three or four pillows. This allowed me some extra comfort and gave me the ability to see my arms and legs often. I refused to have my toes covered as I constantly wanted to monitor them in terms of color. It also enabled me to watch my family and loved ones rub them and around the IV lines and tubes to bring feeling back into my body. Most of my family visited and stayed often. My brother Brian was a constant fixture, and he would rub my forehead for me, which always seemed to be in such intense pain. He would also apply cold washcloths throughout the day. He would also give the best hard pressure foot massages late into the evening to make me feel my feet again and help me sleep. My sister provided much of the same comfort, love, and extra enthusiasm for me. She made me believe that everything was going to be okay. I desperately wanted to believe her, so I allowed myself to internalize her words. They allowed me to keep some semblance of light and hope that I would return to life as normal for my children. They also kept me informed regarding the status of my girls, and they often updated me or brought them to visit me. Their visits provided me with a reason to keep living, a purpose for life. I have a wonderful family!

During my stay there, I was never provided with physical therapy other than a few foot massages or minimal stretches—despite repeated requests from me and my family. A senior physical therapist had explained that it was still too much of a risk to move me to the physical therapy floor. That therapist told me they were doing the best that they could under the circumstances. After many weeks, I was finally allowed to sit in an upright chair approximately twenty minutes. The goal was to incrementally work toward an hour per day. However, in order to move me from my bed to the chair, a crane (called a GOVO machine) had to be used. I would shake violently before the crane was used. This would cause me to hit part of this metal crane with my ankle or foot, which caused bruising and worse: bleeding.

Due to the injuries I would sustain, I was put in a chair only three times during my entire stay at the hospital—and never for longer than thirty minutes. During these times, it seemed so difficult. It seemed like such an effort for the staff to keep me sitting upright. Once I was in a seated position, I would be balanced or "formed" into the chair with folded blankets in every area to support my stability. I would be unable to move from that position for my brief time. Transferring me back to my bed seemed to take more time and effort than the amount of actual time I had spent sitting in the chair or with the physical therapist. Ultimately, the staff began to utilize a bed board for easing my future bed transfers. Again, I was just a name, a buck-a-roo. As such, I became easy to forget by staff.

Thinking back, I am not certain whether I am fortunate or unfortunate to remember most of the details of my traumatic event and hospital stays, particularly the dark details of my stay at the second hospital. I will always remember my first neurologist coming very methodically and purposefully into my room. First, he proceeded to the back of my bed where it was impossible for me to see him. Then, it seemed as if he were moving in slow motion about. It was still difficult to see his full face because he was looking down and would not make eye contact with me. Everything he said during this very first face-to-face consultation sounded like mumblings to me. He continued to look at the ground the entire time as I was lying in my bed, intently focused upon him, while drained and confused at the same time.

Nevertheless, I became increasingly aware as he spoke that he was somewhat familiar with me and my condition. He had performed several observations of me, and he had knowledge of some various movement disorders. Strangely, he had never taken the time to talk to or actually physically examine me before. On this occasion, he quickly and matter-of-factly stated the following: "This is it. You have post-anoxic action myoclonus. Your improvement is going to be minimal." Then he was gone out the door as quick as the wind. My sister gave me a quick grave look and immediately got up to follow the doctor in order to ask questions about my diagnosis. During this brief time, which seemed endless, I took in the firestorm of information that I was just given. I thought about my children. I thought about all the pain, shaking, tremors, and convulsions coupled with the inability to talk, walk, or (most important in my mind) care for my daughters. I could not believe that he had said, "Improvement will be minimal." My brain raced out of control as I thought, *He can't mean forever! He had to be wrong. He did not know me!*

I was somehow able to return from a complete mind spin and thought again to myself (despite his words); *would this symptomology really continue to occur forever? Was this it?* I had continued to think that I was going to just go home and that everything was going to fine—normal!

I immediately felt a surge of uncontrollable rage within me as I saw my sister return with freshly tear-soaked eyes. Unsuccessfully attempting to rip the sheets from on top of me, I released from inside the loudest—yet inaudible— *No!* that I could muster. But because I had no strength or coordination to move on my own—and no voice to be heard—only a flow of tears streamed down my face as I gazed at the recently framed pictures of my girls. I was lying in bed in a state of complete powerlessness. The heart-wrenching pain was both overwhelming and unmanageable. I reached out to my sister with my eyes while looking up and blankly staring around. I saw more pictures of my little girls and friends. I saw all of the colorful cards scattered upon my wall on each side of me. By blinking or whispering to my sister in some fashion, I somehow conveyed to her in my sense of panic, "**This is not it**"!

My legs and arms slowly began to convulse, and then they started to shake rapidly beyond all control. My emotions took over my body. The jerking became painfully obvious to all, and the neurologist who had stood behind me could only nod his head as if affirming that my behavioral actions only confirmed his diagnosis and prognosis. This is not a memory I want etched in my mind. I am sure the same is true for others who have similar trauma stories of their own. This period passed very slowly, and the trauma only became more vivid as a result. Also, though, I became more realistic and accepting of my mortality. My previous thoughts about going home seemed to dissipate.

For the reader – Action Myoclonus is best defined as muscular jerking and convulsions triggered by voluntary movement or an intention to move or possible stimulation. It is worse at attempting precise, coordinated movements. It is the most disabling form of myoclonus and can affect the arms, legs, face, and voice.

At that point, I believed I was worth much more to my children financially (that is, I would have been worth more if I had died). I thought, *"I can't go on living like this—with my pain, symptoms, and the amount of medication I'm taking"*. I felt that the addictive and adverse side effects of the pills were killing me as well. For the first time in my life, I felt like giving up. I wanted to die at times, in my mindless paralyzed state of confusion. This would leave my children with a secure trust and hefty financial future as laid out in my rather timely completed living will. Despite my professional training and self-perceived fathering skills, internally I knew that I would never be able to parent my children again the way I once had. Nor did I want to burden them—my values had already changed.

I had every horrible thought imaginable. I believed I would never be able to parent my children as a capable father, nor "male role model" while strapped to a bed, while having convulsions and tremors that nobody could understand and thus adequately treat. I began to think selfishly about myself and my future. I knew that life for me would be forever changed, and I had some serious "daily" discussions with myself along with meditation sessions and endless prayer. I often lost the battle regarding my own internal debate about my life, and I simply endured the journey that was given to me.

Through diligence and the never-give-up credo that my family support system helped instill and maintain, my natural optimism started to return. I began to believe once again that this was not it—and that I would eventually return to my home with a new place in life ... and a new life to live!

Chapter 5: Hospital III— Rehabilitation!

The third hospital I was sent to seemed to be a rehabilitation "palace" for stroke patients and the like. I soon found there were many eager to evaluate my unique medical condition. Sometime after my arrival, I learned that no one there had seen anyone like me (in terms of symptom severity or complexity) before. After so many hospitals—and after undergoing so much frustration—I was ready for anything or anyone who could make a difference in my life. I knew I should have died previously. It was there I was introduced to a new level of treatment and a pyramid of different doctors and specialists. Initially, one doctor innocently stated, "You should have died with all what happened to you!"

The convulsions continued to be rampant and consistent, and medication cocktails were being mixed, brewed, and tried immediately upon arrival. Daily dosages were being magnified. It was here I was introduced to even more medications and pills that would hopefully help control my convulsions, shakes, pain, and tremors.

At this hospital, I have to say, I was confronted with yet another planet. There was a definite and determined fixed regimen in place for every patient. Because I was such a mystery with an uncommon diagnosis, many medical staff members were anxious to work with me! I was immediately introduced to what my schedule of activities would be for the coming week. I had arrived on a Thursday, late in the afternoon, and I was given until the following Monday to allow for a team to be assembled and a treatment plan coordinated. Until then, I would be further medically assessed, evaluated, medicated and treated.

Shortly after being settled into my room, one individual among many patients stood out. I was told he had been in a horrible accident and had become a paraplegic. He had lost control of all functions of his body, and he was in the bed directly across from mine. He had his mother, wife and children with him often. I knew he was aware of his new existence and of my presence. In my first few days at the hospital, I just lay in bed and traded stares with this man. This went on for hours and hours each day, all day—we were speaking without words! We were speaking with our eyes. I knew he would never move again on his own, and so did he. I wonder if he thought the same about me. I was definitely fearful my path was similar, despite our different diagnoses. We looked the same, we needed the same care, and we were both trauma survivors!

He transferred to his home about a week after I arrived. His entire family was there to support him. They later stated to me upon his discharge that they felt they could better meet his needs at his home with his children. I understood completely! I so wanted to go home as well. I asked a nurse to go home immediately, but I was in no condition to do so. I cried for hours upon his departure because I found myself in the midst of yet another change. I was alone and surrounded by people who were much older (and seemingly dying). None were like me. None looked like me, acted like me, had conditions like me; none could or would communicate with me and my children and family were hours and hours away!

It became apparent that the structure I was to be involved in included very intense physical, occupational, and speech therapy that was to occur six days per week. I was to receive an hour of occupational therapy and an hour of speech therapy daily (with three hours of physical therapy spread throughout the day). I looked forward to this challenge. It was explained to me that I had lost over sixty pounds in a little over two months.

It was well known to my family that I had long before decided to let my hair grow until I could walk again— something I of course was determined to do. It had not been cut in many months, and it was beginning to grow well—despite the medications with its side effect of hair loss. However, after about a week or so, I must say that God sent another angel to me to lift my spirits up and see me through my condition and journey. Again, upon looking into this nurse's eyes, I knew I was safe! She had a charming disposition and positive spirit that struck my core. Not only did she provide a much needed sense of relief and good will, she also convinced me to cut my hair because, in her mind, there was no doubt that I was going to walk again. "Why wait?" she asked! So with all that positive hope flowing in my mind, within my room, I allowed her to cut my hair and shave my beard. My mother was especially thrilled because it showed to her that I finally cared about myself again. This nurse would often visit me to ensure my comfort and safety at the hospital. And she always provided hope! She also later during my stay helped transfer me from my bed into a wheelchair (with assistance from another) from time to time.

I had only seen the outside via a window on rare occasions during my stay there, but I had not been outside, smelled real air or seen the sun in several months. With my family cheering by my side, it was she that wheeled me outside to a patio to see the light of day for the first time after being there for some time. I remember attempting to spread my arms wide while going out the doors of the hospital as if I were on the front of a ship, letting the sun glisten upon me and feeling the gentle breeze blow through my body. I felt an immediate surge of energy. I was strapped in my wheelchair, but I was looking straight into the sun— something I thought I would never do again. It was an amazing, awakening and spiritual moment for all who were there. Some things we just take for granted, but on that day I got a fierce sense of hope and life back! The sun burned deep within me and gave me the sense of having a renewed spirit. God spoke to me as I prayed. Words cannot describe the energy the nurse brought to me each time she entered my room with her sense of "care".

I was very excited at this new hospital facility because there seemed, for the first time, to be hope when I met all the staff. They also brought energy and special and unique care to me. I continued to think that I was actually going to walk out of that facility and return home "normal"— like I was before.

During my entire stay, I was given multiple examinations and more medications to ease my tremor symptoms. I was also given simple and silly daily cognitive tests to test my memory. I soon found the doctors and specialists were finding me a little too special, and their knowledge and handbooks just didn't have me—my specific diagnosis and how to treat it—in there!

Upon my initial physical therapy exam, the physical therapists worked in teams of two and were absolutely wonderful and excited to work with me. There are not enough words to say regarding those young physical therapist's who were so motivational, full of energy, refreshing and consistently positive despite my mood. They made me want to work for them. They were even counselors for me at times—they would always try to listen to me in my unique voice and communication styles and offer sound feedback, while motivating me toward doing my best.

Unfortunately, all that could be done with me initially was to strap me from head to toe on a wooden tilt board and set me up somewhat upright at first. They would gradually increase the angles over time to slowly allow me to gain much needed leg strength and weight. I could not stand at all (or even sit in a chair unaided) for long periods of time because I had no core strength. I had no balance or coordination whatsoever.

They attempted to put me in a wheelchair during this initial period. I nearly fell out at first because I had to be completely strapped inside of it to maintain an upright position. I could not manually move it on my own at first. I was left to try on my own and I stayed in that same place for over two hours. I was in utter disbelief that I needed to be pushed in a wheel chair for the first few weeks until I learned how to use it on my own. It doesn't come with instructions! I had to put my feet in the straps backwards on the foot boards to prevent any of my front tremor leg kicks. It took weeks for me to gain some core strength and ultimately learn how to move that wheelchair forward.

When I could finally use the wheelchair, I moved myself all over that hospital. I later was considered by many nurses to be a crazy driver and I was often asked for my driver's license as I would cruise the hospital halls. There was nothing else to do during down times (other than sit in the room). I'd rather roam the entire hospital! I only had to be belted in (with my feet strapped in to prevent convulsions) while out and about. I often went outside on my own, despite the staff advice as to not to. The sun and patio areas next to my unit I found were just beautiful to ignore. Perspective is everything!

As stated, the physical therapists there were all bright, energetic, and knowledgeable in terms of the needs of trauma—they just didn't know how to treat my form of myoclonus. It was foreign to them. However, unlike what I had previously experienced, they worked with me as though I were an intelligent human being ... an actual person! I was able to communicate somewhat now because my tracheotomy had been removed quickly after arrival. The removal of my tracheotomy was done the initial weekend I was there so that I could participate in physical therapy that following week. Without it, I was able to push some words out with air. More often than not I'm sure, the words were inaudible. Hand, body, and physical signs were my main methods of communication I found most effective.

During the latter part of my second to third week, I was transferred to a therapy mat slightly above the ground. This was to test different areas and parts of my body to assess mobility, strength, general movement and determine the triggers which caused some tremors. The tests were also used to design and redesign an overall treatment plan for me.

I was initially shocked that I couldn't lift my back or behind off the mat in any way. I couldn't turn myself over on the mat of my own accord. I couldn't do a push-up that would lift my nose up off the mat or a sit up or leg raise. I was simply just a body that initially could not move. I could not believe how little muscle, coordination, and control I had and had lost. By this time, I had lost over seventy pounds in just over three months. I went from being 230 solid pounds to a 160 pound body of atrophy. I remember thinking I use to do 50 push ups so easy and bench press over 400 pounds - What happened?

I remember a following initial work-out and trying so hard to do a little sit up, and the sweat just poured from me due to the effort. I tried to raise my lower back from the mat an inch... an inch, but all that happened was I raised one foot a few inches off the mat in an uncontrolled reflex. I lay there practicing spreading my fingers and lifting my arms, legs, and head day after day for hours, days, weeks and months the entire time I was there. It was humbling.

There were timelines for every activity. I struggled each morning. I was pushed by physical therapists beyond what I thought my body could take. Often I would inadvertently kick one of my physical therapists due to a particular stretch and a subsequent tremor. It became a game somewhat, but it was a game of pain and torture that was not fun in any way. Each effort to stretch my body, leg, abs, or shoulders shook many other parts of my body. I was stunned that I could not touch my ankles in any way—nor did I have the strength to do a simple backbend after being so physically strong and active all my life. Each day was a full work-out. I still remember the warm sweat and smell that clung to the mat afterwards.

As I sat on the mat being stretched for long periods, my mind would often get lost in another time. I would create my own happy place! I would reflect upon my children. I would also drift into times when my brother and I would go golfing, and I would mentally walk every hole of several different courses I had etched in my mind. In my head, we would walk and talk while I would strike the ball— perfectly, of course. I would also daydream, at times, of kayaking while remembering every tree, turn, twist and rock of my favorite class III river. But yet best of all, the memories that floated through my mind were those of "fatherhood"—including sharing all the special times and mindful strolls down memory lane with my children. And then it was on to the next stretch or exercise.

In the latter part of the third week, I was stood up between two full body mats with three physical therapists assisting. One was in front, one was behind me, and another was there for assistance as I was squeezed between the two mats for support in a standing position. I tried to stand for nearly a week straight on my own, but to no avail. However, the hours of rehabilitation I spent daily served to promote both my body and mind development. And the rehabilitation served as a reminder for me that I was afflicted with a very serious condition.

It appeared that every other patient who came in at or around the same time as I was improving—using walkers and canes or simply walking—and I couldn't even generate enough power to move myself in a wheelchair at times. As my hopes for walking out of the hospital wavered, I remember laughing and thinking that it didn't look like I was going to play in the annual Turkey Bowl that year that was coming up. Though I laughed, I realized then that I also wasn't going to get to do many things I was accustomed to doing. There is just so many to list. It was humbling.

As stated, many of the doctors and physical therapists were excellent. Despite the fact that it was only a short-term rehabilitation facility, they agreed to keep working with me due to my overall determination and signs of improvement.

However, I was still somewhat paralyzed, and I had no basic core control whatsoever. When a pillow was removed from my head, my head would gently fall back after a few seconds. I would practice simple head raises for hours and hours, and over time, I improved. However, at times, if I was not carefully balanced or strapped into extremely tightened sheets, I would fall out of my bed or lean over and crash into something. This, unfortunately, occurred more than a few times—despite having bars on my bed. However, over time, I improved. I gained better strength to sit up on my own with the daily grind of constant practice and the use of hanging hospital bed bars. I would use these to practice pull-ups daily, and I used flex bands for extra strength work after physical therapy throughout each waking day.

It was there I met the second neurologist. From what I recall, I immediately requested consultation with him upon arrival to discuss further, what I had heard so prematurely earlier. During my first consultation (that occurred the second week I was there), he unbelievably and ineptly told me the same thing: "This is it." This time, I was seated in a wheelchair and heavily dosed on medications. He spoke to me as though I were a six-year-old child rather than a grown, educated man who remembers everything. I remember distinctly that he stated, "Mr. Green, this is it. You will need full-time care." He continued to say that he believed I would be on the medications I was taking for the rest of my life, which was a second major hit to me at the time. Another movement disorder neurologist I saw later said, "You are in uncharted territory." He was referring to the high dosages of medications I was taking. I was still the experimental patient—no one was looking at the potential consequences.

I had once envisioned simply going home. Now I would take any pill or amount of pills that would allow me to go home in the body that I first had before this trauma and treatment that started back in June. However, that was not to be. I was on symptom management medications that allowed hope. But the number and quantity of medications I had been introduced to during my stay greatly concerned me. I wasn't better in my mind!

Although the hospital strived to help me from the very beginning, the care (at times, from some) was questionable. As my time for discharge drew near, I felt that the team was rushing to try to teach me many things of great importance. One such skill was the ability to transition from a wheelchair to a bed and vice versa; or to feed myself—something I had not done in over three months since my asthma attack; or to dress myself, which was a near-impossible task given my tremors. It seemed they also rushed to teach me how to transition from my wheelchair to a shower seat and vice versa. We even went outside and utilized a car to practice transitioning in and out of my wheelchair. This basically entailed me being picked up and strapped in. I never was able to accomplish this task (or many others) while there.

I remember being in an occupational therapy room for weeks upon weeks and attempting to move a tiny square block along a simple little wire (like the toys you see at a doctor's or dentist's office). I never could accomplish that silly task during my stay, and that frustrated me. It was amazing how much concentration and coordination I put forth to move a tiny little bead or block along a wire. And it was upsetting that such an activity would create such a challenge for me that I would tremor or shake and ultimately fail. I felt as though the occupational therapist pretty much gave up on me after the second or third week instead of trying to help me progress. She had me do the same things over and over for the remaining weeks I was there—despite my request to be moved to a new occupational therapist. It was clear she had no passion or care for her patients. She appeared to be more consumed by the clock than the act of helping me or anyone else. So I sat there with blocks and beads and wires to move about. It was humbling.

In speech therapy, I just remember crying for weeks. I simply could not talk. My voice after the tracheotomy had been removed was simply gone ... never to return to what it used to be. To better understand, with action myoclonus, for every *action* one may do, there may be a ripple effect of tremors and shakes through ones body being the *myoclonus*. With the action of speaking, I would feel tremors throughout my throat and upper body that, at times, prevented speech. To the average person, I guess I would look as if I were fighting to say words from a mouth that at times couldn't speak. My mind was always five sentences ahead of my mouth. I had unseen tremors occurring in my vocal cords. When my voice did come forth, my tone, pitch, and sound were completely different. The speech therapist was very compassionate and good. She tried her best as I was re-taught how to form words with my tongue and mouth despite my condition. She tried various techniques with me, but it seemed our hellos took up the whole time.

At one point during my time with this therapist, I became very upset with my situation and my voice. She recorded me reading a short passage in a magazine. I could not believe what I was hearing. It sounded like something out of a horror movie, and I could not believe it was actually me. I was sent into total shock! I actually wanted to break the recorder. I was so disturbed that I had the therapist call my personal cell phone number to listen to my old cell phone greeting to hear my "real" voice. She put the phone on speaker phone so we could both hear and huddled over it. I think we both cried as a result, and my session was over.

After extending my stay at the hospital by several weeks, I was told I would be discharged on a specific date. I had so many unmet goals. I had put in big letters, "I will not leave until I walk" above my bed upon arrival several months before. I believed that I was going to walk. So learning I was leaving unable to walk, talk, or do many other things was very disturbing. It appeared I was going home strapped in a wheelchair (in dire need of constant care). My coordination was that of a nine-month-old baby—I could barely crawl and talk, and I could not stand on my own. I could not touch the top of my head or brush my teeth without causing bleeding or serious injury due to my action myoclonus. I could not hold a cup without spilling its contents or dress myself without assistance due to my tremors. *What am I to do? I wondered?*

Toward the latter part of my stay there, I was fed with the assistance of a nurse (after my stomach tube had been unexpectedly and painfully removed). I will never forget the doctor who came into my room to say he was there to clean my stomach tube area. He quickly asked me my first name and surprisingly ripped the tube right out of my stomach with his hand. It felt as though I had been shot when this surprise guest pulled the tube out. Blood is the first word that comes to mind. I bled for hours.

I remember when they put the tube line in. A doctor put something in my mouth so I would not bite down and lifted me up so I could watch on an HD screen what was being done to me. He then began to put a wire tube down my throat and into my stomach. He pierced my stomach with it and cut a hole a few inches above my belly button while I was fully alert. I could not believe it was happening! I thought I was going to see something really cool, but experienced something far more disturbing. As he pulled the tube from my "new" belly button, the other end of the tube went down my throat and into my stomach. It had some form of butterfly hook that made it secure and allowed for feeding. I now realize that, had he given me warning, I would never have let him do it (without a morphine drip at least).

Looking back on my stay (including nearly two months of additional, extensive in-patient rehabilitation services), I see that I went from lying motionless in a bed to being propped up by a tilt board, to using therapy mats, to sitting in a wheelchair on my own, to ultimately using a walker at times (with help) toward the end. I believe they did their job. It was truly a wellness facility for me—hope was provided for my internal soul. I remember being there at first and watching my body twitch in an extreme manner. I remember being bombarded by specialists and physical therapists who all wanted to work with a survivor of acute action myoclonus. I also remember scarring staff initially with my uncontrollable tremors and movements. At one point, as I reflect, my knee hit my head, and I could not be contained until strapped into a bed.

I was a challenge for many staff. During my treatment there, I also remember being nicknamed *"Frogger"* by the physical therapy staff due to my uncontrollable forward thrusting tremors and convulsions. On more than one occasion—even with the best physical therapists by my side—I would thrust forward off a mat or worse. Once, during a new workout in which I was lying on a floor mat, I had a tremor, thrust forward, and went straight through the wall in front of me head first. My body lunged forward, and my head stuck in the wall as my body twitched uncontrollably. It was a quite a sight for all to see.

I was aware that, whenever I transitioned to a bed from a wheelchair and back, I always had two people there to support me. Outside of the hospital, there would be no one. The day prior to leaving the hospital, I canceled all of my scheduled activities that were planned. I lay in bed and cried the entire day. *Overwhelming* is the only word that comes to mind when I remember each physical therapist coming in to gently and warmly hug me. I remember lying in bed and looking at all the pictures and words of hope taped on my wall. I felt as though my life was spinning away from me once again, and I was thinking about all my unmet expectations. The reality of my trauma again sank in—this time a little deeper – a little darker! No one knew what was ahead for me and most importantly, myself. It was an extremely frightening thought.

Chapter 6: Reflections on an Early Discharge—I Still Cannot Walk?

Upon discharge, I was scheduled to meet with a movement disorder specialist. It appeared to be set. He had been specifically assigned to my very unique case after much debate.

However, prior to my discharge, there had been a medical discharge, family team meeting to arrange and discuss my overall care and treatment needs upon my release. During this meeting, my family was stunned and extremely vocal that more was not being done. They were unhappy that there were only minimal plans in place to further assist me upon release. They were shocked that I was being sent home when I was "board and care" material.

This discharge meeting became adversarial. My family vocally supported my rights to see a specialist. I remember my brother laughing after hearing the team's plan for my discharge. He commented to the doctor in charge, "If he had a foot problem, I wouldn't send him to a shrink ... I'd send him to where he needs to go, a Podiatrist! Why can't you all send my brother to where he needs to go?" It took only a few minutes of discussion with my family before the medical discharge team decided that, upon my release, I would be referred to a movement disorder specialist. I was told there were only three in California who were also affiliated with my insurance network. I chose the one closest to my home. An appointment was made for the day of my release.

Other aftercare plans were being made by my family within my own home. Additional services were being looked into within my own county. After so long in the hospital, my own funds were getting very low. I had not earned a paycheck in many months. My savings were being rapidly depleted due to medical bills, typical expenses, and for my children. The idea of me working anytime soon was out of the question. I went on SSDI and Medi-Cal for my children, but I had to liquidate and exhaust every single asset I had prior to being qualified. It took nearly eight to nine months before I was accepted. It was very humbling.

In any case, on the day of my discharge, I was transported by ambulance to a major area hospital (approximately an hour away). It had been arranged that my family would be there to greet me, help me through the initial consultation meeting, and transport me home! After all the months of hospitalizations, medical speculation, near-death experiences and (most painfully of all) being away from my children, all I wanted was to go home!

I never wanted to allow myself to believe "this was it"—despite all the cloudy days I may have had. I always believed the sun would shine again for me. I had great faith! I was an athlete just a few months prior and thought I was too active, mentally strong, and resilient to accept things as they were. I continued my refusal to accept what my reality was, and I continued to imagine what it was going to be like in the future.

I was aware I had died and come back to life, as they say. I knew my health was not good as a result of the asthma attack and diagnosis, but I began to feel immortal again. I was convinced I would somehow get back to my normal life. I never realized how humbled I would become, and I never realized how many adjustments would be made to my life (and to the lives of others) as far as parenting, family, friends, career, finances, children, activities, home, future, and overall placement in the world just to name a few. Although I didn't know what anoxic action myoclonus was at the time, I didn't really care either! All I knew was that the doctors didn't know me or my inner strength. Despite the diagnosis, I knew I would someday become well and prove the doctors wrong!

When I finally arrived to see the movement specialist, there appeared to be a mix up regarding my appointment. The movement specialist, I was told, would not be starting for another month. There I sat, alone in the waiting room with no one to sign me in after the ambulance ride. However, because of the months of hospitalization I endured and my current condition, the chief of neurology (who knew about me) wanted to see me right away. He wanted to conduct an assessment prior to the movement disorder specialist's arrival and offer his opinion. This happened as my mother and Craig arrived. After a series of what I thought to be strange questions and some physical tests, he immediately ordered a new MRI. He then confirmed my diagnosis of action myoclonus. After a few more tests, I heard the words *Lance-Adams syndrome* for the first time.

I remember, at the end of our meeting, he asked me to grab a dime from the palm of his hand. I refused to participate in this antic, partially because I didn't want my mother to see what the doctor and I both knew to be true: I could not complete this silly task. I could not grab a dime. My hand was not coordinated enough at that point, and had I tried, I would have shaken and probably knocked the dime from his palm. I was embarrassed, and I wanted to get away from him and go home. After the doctor answered some more of my mother's questions, we set out to leave. As he attempted to shake my convulsing hand, he crushed my inner heart without knowing it when he uttered the familiar words: "This is it, Mr. Green." I was wheeled out from the fourth hospital with those words echoing between my ears.

Chapter 7: Reflections on My Care—Let's Put Back the Care in Care!

In this journey of mine, I wanted to focus on many things at the start. I mainly wanted to help others through my experience because I *care*! I never knew my life, mind and words would be led back to that word so readily. Passion for my caring comes from "caring" for others and the horrific treatment I received from some medical staff. They did not care for me. I've shared some personal thoughts on the torturous and inept care I received from some doctors, specialists, RNs, and others.

Witnessing death is unforgettable. Witnessing firsthand the reactions of supposedly caring hospital employees after the death of an "unwanted patient" was incredible. From what I witnessed, the families who were not present were never notified in a timely manner. What was done by the medical staff to cover up any mishaps was unconscionable. And the deceased patient's roommates often had to sit through some terrible experiences ... without a voice in my case! It was excruciating to see humor displayed by several staff members before and after a patient's death. Other patients observing this behavior seemed equally appalled.

Sometimes, the length of time between the death of a patient and a call to the doctor or family member was alarming. It seemed to take forever! I was shocked and surprised that the medical team tried to clean up the facial and body area only minutes prior to the arrival of the doctor or family. It seemed like a routine procedure. Gruesomely, each body remained in the same condition after the family departed. Curtains were not drawn for the benefit of the other patients in the room. We only had a corpse to look at, and in my case, to pray over! This disturbing behavior was so unbecoming. I saw this occur on two different shifts, and these events were frightening to all who witnessed them (including those in a very fragile condition, like me). I was scared and in need of consistent critical "care".

It's a war zone in a hospital! I found one generally has to battle for his or her life in the very place where one expects to receive quality care, help, and sanctuary. Based upon my experience, we need dramatic reform in the health *care* system. Those in charge of our loved ones need to be held accountable.

I can never forget the disturbing look in the eyes of the doctors, neurologists, and other medical staff members who I refer to as terrorist nurses. They intimidate you, promote fear in you, and abuse you mentally and physically. These episodes have scarred my soul forever.

These are the nurses who might win the love of your family when interacting with them. But when your family is gone, so are they—and so is the care! There were too many nurses who physically or psychologically harmed me. They drugged me and tortured me. I was provided indelible looks that screamed: "I don't care." The absolute lack of true care from those I thought were highly trained professionals was astounding.

There are so many instances I could write about, as stated before. One that comes to mind involves my buzzer going off in my room due to the IV bags coming in contact with it, and the nurse tilting me upside down until my toes were dangling above my head. I was helpless. I remember her warning me not to hit the button as I passed out. There were many similar encounters. Thus, *be there for your loved one!*

I want to go back to the look in the eyes of so many specialists and nurses. In time, I noticed a difference in some. They displayed a blank stare when looking at me or performing a task on me. I could always tell who cared and who didn't by their eyes (and behavior, of course). Sometimes, I felt there was an absolute "I am the expert" or "don't-question my attitude" stance within the doctors and nurses who rotated weekly and knew nothing about me, but a chart at the foot of my bed. As stated previously, I could see some read my notes and quickly moved on with no emotion at all. Some who read my notes stayed a little longer and seemingly really wanted to learn more about my condition—after all, my condition is extremely rare. But, they didn't offer ideas, opinions or treatment suggestions. They shook their head and moved on!

I can never forget my experiences in the hospitals—the pictures and words are etched into my mind. Far too many doctors, nurses, and care providers within the medical field provided me with memories that have left me with something like post-traumatic stress disorder. And, of course, that disorder accompanies my previous traumatic event! Again, an important message that I want to impart is that you can't trust everyone to provide high-quality care.

My training in college toward becoming a therapist—and the training I received from my parents—leads me to try to help others in need and stick up for those who need help. This was certainly not what I experienced! I am not stating that this is true in all cases—I did meet some wonderful medical treatment staff, but not as many as I would have hoped to meet! In short, I can't say it loud enough to the family and friends of a trauma survivor: <u>Be there!</u> Be the presence. Be the voice for that loved one who may not have a means of communicating with you!

Chapter 8: Reflections on Coming Home—A New World!

Gender is a defining aspect of self in our everyday lives—specifically in our social lives. I believe that, in a trauma situation, gender can sometimes become *uniquely, unique.* That is to say, as a male, I desperately felt the need to be a "man" – to show strength and begin my new life and try to start over. I was also in need of a grief period, but was not given this opportunity initially to adequately grieve. I now question the freedom newly disabled and traumatized individuals are given to return to what was once normalcy. As stated, this can be especially difficult for males (and women) I think thrust back into their old prescribed roles. They may not be prepared for roles such as father, boyfriend, caregiver, worker, leader, supporter, protector, head of household, etc. I was not mentally ready for any roles other than simply adjusting and transitioning to a life outside of an ICU hospital room.

I believe gender for women is also very defining and can be crippling for trauma survivors and the perceived disabled. Yet, I find society generally may have a more compassionate stance toward woman and may even promote a more positive persona and even help generate or create increased opportunities to find their "woman-hood" within; versus assisting a man toward finding his "man-hood" again.

For example, I see TV shows depicting men in wheel-chairs playing an often violent sport creating chaos placing value on the strength, power and control of these men. I also see another show depicting women in wheel chairs specific to placing value on their sex appeal and building and gaining self worth and independence. What a difference in the value we place on what it means to be a "man" or what it means to be a "woman" in society... let alone in the world of trauma and the disabled.

Coming home, at first, I was not even prepared to sleep in my own bed without assistance. I was also not emotionally prepared for the sudden feeling of loneliness. When alone, I felt my disabilities and inabilities become magnified. That first evening—despite my deep desire to go home—I felt even more completely vulnerable. I wasn't able to sleep on my stomach due to the presence of saturation that resulted from being on my back and lying still for so long. The pain I felt when I tried to turn over was stunning. My upper torso would often just collapse in because I was unable to turn over.

However, my coming home indeed felt just like a celebration! At first I was as joyous as anybody could possibly be. I had just survived a trauma. This was a miracle! But I was unable to prepare myself for the major adaptations required of me. How could anybody prepare for the unexpected?

I felt like the main character in *Born on the Fourth of July* when he returns home from the war in his wheelchair. In the movie, there is a scene where he is driven down the street to his home. Everyone sees him sitting in his seat, so they greet him normally at first. However, once the character is out of the car and his family and acquaintances see the fragility of his once capable body and his subsequent struggle within his wheelchair, nobody quite knows how to act. Further, nobody really knows how to look at him, touch him, or respond to him. In his new situation, the character is actually unable to respond to others as well. I can understand this character very well because I experienced that scene when I came home.

In my case, I was lifted out of my car by my brother and placed into my wheelchair for all my supporters to see. I was then pushed through my house and given a tour. My brother had dramatically and thoughtfully customized my home while I was away to try to fit my many new and unknown needs. It was another shock that I only weighed 157 pounds (down from a fit, strong and proud 230 pounds!).

My brother had done both an amazing and inspiring job adapting and improving my entire home for me. He focused all his experience and thoughts upon my potential special needs, such as wider hallways and doorframes for my wheelchair. He made custom ramps to create a single level throughout my house, and he created a physical therapy room (which he modeled after the hospitals). Each bathroom was remodeled so I could use them independently (we had spent time imagining and planning the bathrooms with some of the medical staff beforehand). However, there was still so much unknown to me about the new situation. I wondered how I would cook, eat, sleep, bathe, and so on. Again, how can one really prepare oneself or another for coming home after a trauma? I believe it is possible if you are thoughtful and seek support. Most of all, I believe that, over time and through learned experiences, a new life may emerge!

In time, it became apparent that the area where I needed the most help was eating. So I was fed. Eventually, I learned I would need bars in every room in my home for standing stability. One room in desperate need of such bars was my bathroom. The bars were required so that I could hold them independently and have the freedom to use and do things that I hadn't thought about or did on my own previously. A shower bench alone wasn't enough without the assistance of my brother. However, with the shower bars that he modified for me, an independent shower was possible. Asking for and receiving help was extremely important!

My county insurance allowed for an in-home physical therapist to come into my home once a week until a determination was made that I was physically stable. This only lasted for four short weeks upon my return home. My brother was amazingly supportive and generally tried his best to be there at all times. I had nothing but time, and I worked out constantly. When the therapist was there, he must have thought I was improving rapidly on my own or he was an amazing therapist. From his demeanor, I know I must have looked pretty strong compared to some of the other county patients he had.

When he did show for his scheduled four appointments, he was only able to stay approximately thirty minutes. Although I didn't think it was time for any form of help to end, he indicated on the fourth appointment that I had demonstrated enough improvement for services to end. He said that despite the fact that I still had very limited movement, experienced consistent and powerful tremors, and could not stand or be left alone. Once again, I was left in fear that no professional would be following my improvement or helping me improve. My family was my divine intervention and salvation! They lifted my spirits daily when I was down, and they kept me floating with hope despite my trials.

After my county assistance ended, my brother moved in with me for nearly a year to help care for me and my children. He saw my life through his eyes: my pain, my grief, my sweat, my falls, my broken bones and my blood. I believe he lived a part of it with me. After all, he addressed my needs twenty-four hours per day, seven days per week. Over time, as he helped inspire me to improve, his hands-on assistance was needed less and less. However, my falls and accidents increased as his presence decreased as well. I love my brother dearly, and I am very grateful to him for giving a part of his life to me every day for nearly a year! I am so grateful for all in my family who inspired me and gave their unconditional love and care to and for me over the years!

As for my mother, she is an absolute angel! She is an amazing, creative, and giving Renaissance woman who is able to accomplish anything she sets her mind to. I cannot say enough words to describe her—she is a very big motivating factor in the strength behind this book. I don't think I could have continued, grieved, or healed without her love. She is the most incredible person I know! When I am asked about (or think about) how I made it through my trauma with such optimism, I always say that the credit goes to her. My mother has provided love in some small or large way every day. She drives to my home regularly to ensure that all of my personal needs are met. She has done this every week for the past five years—despite living nearly two hours away. She is truly my hero!

Looking back over the first six to nine months after returning home, I can see that adapting to my new body was very difficult—harder and more complex than anyone could have been able to prepare me for. My brother and I used my own therapy mat daily, and he slowly began to help me push my body harder than what I believed I was capable of. The medications did help. The tremors and shakes were lessened, and I was improving in all areas. Yet my tremors were still very powerful and present throughout the day. There were only brief and specific slots of time that I was able to walk with the assistance of both a walker and my brother. Initially, his help prevented me from tipping sideways, backwards or forward. Later, I stabilized the walker with weights, and that stopped me from falling backward. The added weight also helped me gain needed strength as I pushed the walker. At the same time, my brother held onto a belt strap that was tied firmly around my waist to help keep me standing upright and prevent me from falling.

It was several months after arriving home that I was finally able to meet the movement specialist. I was anticipating our meeting with much excitement, but upon meeting him, the first question he posed to me as he came into the examining room was, "Why are you in a wheelchair?" This took me by surprise because it appeared to me that he hadn't yet read what was in his hand, and he didn't seem to have any knowledge of my condition. I had already done hundreds of hours of extensive research on my own by that time, and I had long anticipated this meeting with him. I had many questions for a professional I hoped could help me—someone who knew about my condition, someone who actually understood action myoclonus.

Upon hearing his question, I felt like I was being punched in the stomach. It took my breath away for a moment. I stared at him blankly and gathered my thoughts for what seemed like several minutes before I was able answer in some fashion that I was unable to walk. He seemed surprised and immediately began discussing his knowledge of the condition I suffered from, but not my particular case. It seemed as if he hadn't yet reviewed my medical file. After hearing him speak for a while, I noted that he did appear bright. Like most neurologists, he spoke in generalities regarding the first year for myoclonus patients. He stated that patients usually attained a maximum recovery within a year (he called it the optimal development period). He further reported that each of the myoclonus patients that he had worked with previously had walked eventually.

This made me wonder why I wasn't able to, but it gave me great hope that one day I would!

All I can say is that I left that appointment with some modicum of hope. He was the first neurologist I worked with who didn't say, "This is it!" I went to see him twice following that initial appointment. Unfortunately, each visit was less positive and less productive than the previous one. His energy, outlook and attention seemed to decrease, and he seemed much less actively involved in my case. His medical team displayed the same uncaring attitude and gave me the same sense of "care" that my previous caregivers provided.

So what actually happened on June 8, 2006? I was told the medical reasoning, but I was still confused as to how an asthma attack could have possibly caused all of the hardship—not only for me, but for all those who cared for me as well!

I grieved daily as I adapted to my new life. But I also had my children with me to help me maintain what I refer to as my "sobriety of life." As I stated, I was also incredibly fortunate to have rotating family members helping to ensure my safety and to conserve my daily will for life. As a disabled survivor of trauma, I found that there was really no time to adapt. I was once the best at fathering my girls, but it was hard to take charge and do that job as effectively. It felt like they had to parent me at times. I became even more traumatized in many ways after the event. After losing my body, I lost my career, many of the people who called themselves my friends, all of my money, my material items, many goals and part of me. Ultimately,

I lost my "control" of my children. I lost everything I once had, including the home where I had raised my girls. My traumatic event even hindered my ability to parent the children I helped create!

As stated above, because my disability was so crippling initially, it was impossible to live alone or be the very capable single parent I once was. To be honest, at that point, I just was not able to cope mentally, emotionally, or physically with my lack of recovery. I have a great family and loved ones who have always supported me, but the negative prognosis and daily grind of my treatment and internal thinking left me in despair. Living with depression is difficult for anybody, but it seemed especially cruel because I had to live in the same body as before. I continued to cry in private daily while trying to maintain an exterior of hope for the world to see. My goal was to ignore my own emotional needs and work solely at being there for my children and adhering to an arduous physical therapy and speech regimen. I did this daily; I did this religiously! I believed!

It was no surprise to anybody that, from the moment I came home, I tried to walk. Alas, I generally fell daily. Due to the fact that I had lost so much weight, I had to be carried by my brother at times. I weighed what I did in 8th or 9th grade initially. It was still too difficult to maintain balance—even while sitting on the floor, even while propped up with pillows with a hand supporting my back. I had completely lost my muscle core! I used my therapy mat daily—sometimes all day. I utilized rubber cords to stretch and further test my new and very foreign body. With each new flex, I twitched and shook, but I learned how to adapt to my tremors. I also began to get strong and regain much-needed weight. Surprisingly, I found that lifting heavy weights grounded me if I was counterbalanced with something as heavy as I was. It also helped to improve my tremors and overall body muscle and mass. I was gaining my weight back quickly.

Despite my adventurous efforts at self-rehabilitation during my first year home, no one could have prepared me for my lack of independence. I could not do anything without the help of another, and I realized how truly dependent I was. While trying to feed myself, I would draw blood with the utensils or drop plates. I tried to shower alone, but even with a handicapped bench, I would fall into the shower walls or floor. One time, I fell through a glass shower door. I lay there for hours in the tub and bled as tremors raced through my body. I slowly picked all of the glass out of my body before I attempted to move again. Another time, I had a major tremor and fell—rolled down, really—twenty-four stairs. My unfortunate brother was in tow, trying to catch me. I remember my head landing *smack* on the concrete floor at the end of the stairs. I dislocated my shoulder, broke a rib, and deeply cut my head during that tumble. My brother had to be rushed to the hospital for a deep wound on his head that came from the wheelchair.

In the first two years, I broke over fifteen bones. Each break has a different, unique, and bloody story. To date, I've fallen hundreds of times. But most importantly: *I've risen each time!* I've had multiple fractures, concussions, and hundreds of stitches and staples. I've had countless injuries that should have been stitched up, stapled shut, or given medical attention ... but were not. Let me state for the record that walking is so under-rated by those who are able to do so easily and so valued by those who can't. Perception is everything!

There are so many stories about my recovery. Some are of an emotional nature; some are physical; some are mental; and some are even hysterical. One book is incapable of holding all that I have experienced. However, I will try to mention the stories that are relevant to this journey and story.

For nearly a year, the simple act of moving from a wheelchair to a bed, chair, couch, car, etc. was nearly impossible without the help of others. My core strength didn't come back for at least a year, so I was unable to transfer from car to wheelchair or *vice versa*. However, through determination and experience, I learned to adapt to meet my ever-changing needs. I began to use my ankles, knees, shoulders, elbows, hands, and head to make transitions—and life—easier. Adapting and trying new things became a new way of life.

For instance, my electric shaver previously got the best of me. It was like a loose machine running rampant on my face. I learned to lay my head on a towel upon my bathroom counter sink. I would balance myself in my wheel-chair and with one arm use my electric shaver (and give in to any shakes). Some small tremors even assisted in this process. It worked! I also used to wedge my arm in a corner of my sink with a towel and use an electric toothbrush to work around my gums and teeth very carefully. Although there would be blood more often than not, I felt empowered doing this on my own.

Life became a routine of my own devising. I learned to put my clothes on in my bed and slip in and out of them while on my mattress before getting up and moving about. I learned to do this about an hour or so after medications were taken bedside (medications that had been set out the night before). All of my shirts and any pants with buttons had been given away because I could not fasten the buttons without accidently ripping them off. I also got rid of all my shoes with laces because I couldn't tie them.

One routine that got easier was eating. I learned to smash or blend many different meals in a juicer and drink them out of a large sippy cup.

The best rehabilitation I did for myself was joining the local YMCA. I had the luxury of a scooter to transport myself after I had practiced many times going back and forth from my home. It was a little over a mile to the gym, but it got me out of my house and removed my sense of isolation. It also allowed the sun to touch my face and renew my spirit. I would work out vigorously with weights and then went into the therapy pool for an aqua-aerobics class mainly utilized by senior citizens. My daily intent and focus was to walk in that four-foot, indoor, heated therapy pool. Of course, the first few attempts resulted in me leaning a certain way, losing my balance, and tipping over. On some of my first visits, I would have drowned if someone wasn't near (I made sure someone was near). Over time, I was able to accomplish quite a lot in the pool.

However, thinking back, I know I scared quite a few of those seniors at first. I was once a very strong and capable swimmer, and I thought initially that balancing and floating only a few months post-release would be easy. However, I soon learned that was beyond my capabilities! I will never forget being the youngest in a group of what appeared to be regulars and seeing the looks of concern on their faces when they first saw me. Some even came up to me and prayed for and with me without knowing me or anything about me. The kindness of strangers is an amazing thing at times! Whatever the emotion was that I inspired in some, it appeared there existed compassion for a young man on a scooter who could barely walk or talk. There was compassion for a man who shook violently while trying to get into the water, but was still determined to do so. Once in the warm water, I knew that all eyes were on me every time. Apparently, I was always much more confident in my abilities than they were!

I remember the first time I was actually in the water and bumped into the group leader by accident. It made me feel anxious and threw me off balance. I went under the water, unable to stand up. While under water, it was amazing to me that I could not find my legs to stand—nor did I have the strength to even float. In seconds, I had seemingly ten sets of hands (in places they probably should not have been) pulling me up to the surface. Once upright, the group leader pretty much ordered me to the edge of the pool where there were handicapped bars for me to hold on to. I took her advice. From that moment on, my improvement was obvious for all to see.

Over the course of time, I slowly began to walk in the water, lap after lap. Then I began swimming long distances with determination. After that first to second year, I began to swim approximately 2–3 miles per week in the 25-meter lap pool and walk approximately 1–2 miles per week in the 20-meter therapy pool. I felt that this was truly the beginning of my comeback.

I acquired yet another nickname—I became known as the "Cadillac Man" because I rode my scooter to the gym regularly. One day, I tried to do a U-turn near the pool to prepare for my lap swimming (as I had done so many times before). For some unknown reason, I had a brief tremor, and my scooter plunged into the pool—into the deep end—with me still holding onto the handlebars. With an apparent smile on my face, I sank twelve feet down to the bottom of the pool, totally confused about what just happened. Once at the bottom, I let go, swam up, and got out of the pool on my own. The young lifeguard on duty appeared to have a heart attack and took some time to ponder what had just happened. There was one swimmer in the pool at that time who took charge of the situation. He helped the lifeguard push my scooter out of the 25-meter lap pool. They brought it from the deep end into the shallow end and eventually out of the pool completely. From then on, I was known to one and all as "Titanic Man". Another moniker … great!

A few months later, I was fortunate enough to acquire a new scooter that was much faster than the old one. One day, after returning home from the gym, I was cut off by a speeding car and ended up flipping my scooter. The car never stopped, and the scooter landed on top of me, of course. Bystanders were able to get the scooter off and help me stand up. I cleaned up the scrapes, bruises, and blood! I rode my new scooter home with a fractured wrist. As I rode home, I listened to the sound of the ambulance siren racing to the scene. By the time it arrived on the scene, I was long gone. I wanted to be home!

I soon felt that I could walk on a treadmill, and I was able to get one for my therapy room. The initial setting was the lowest the machine had: .06 mph and I was able to stay on for about 20 minutes. I slowly worked my way up to 2.0 mph for an hour during year two. I was also able to use a walker on my own outside with greater mobility and stability for short distances.

I can vividly remember the first walk that I took with my walker without being weighed down or having anyone by my side. There was a green garbage can that I made my goal—it was about 100 yards or so down the street. It took about forty-five minutes each way for me to make that trip, but that first walk made me feel triumphant!

For the average person, a walker may seem like an easy transition. However, for a person who actually has to hold the walker, learn how to use it, and adapt it to his or her particular disability, every leaf, rock, crack, bump, tree root, piece of glass, cigarette butt, piece of garbage, etc. is a challenging obstacle. I always tried to walk on the grassy side of the sidewalk or park because, more often than not, I fell. But as my mother told me, "Brett, if you want to walk … walk!" During those arduous walks and falls, I also thought of every neurologist who had said, "This is it!" I wanted to walk. Sinclair Lewis said, "Fail. Fail again. Fail better." This I did masterfully, but I would keep on trying.

Nearly a year to the date after my trauma, I was interviewed and ultimately rehired for my old position as a family court mediator. This was a major milestone for me. It was unbelievable that I could come back from such an event and regain some sense of my life. However, I soon realized that, due to my disability (as opposed to my ability); I was being forced out of that position. I was treated so differently by most—no question. Although I feel no resentment toward my fellow coworkers—I love them dearly—when I noticed this treatment, it was a major setback to my overall recovery and emotional healing process. I firmly believe (and it is proven by my records) that I can do the job as well as any, but I did not earn back the confidence of my peers. I was seen purely as a disabled person. I was viewed as a charity case! Nobody bothered trying to see past my disability to *me*. Nobody bothered to notice that, cognitively, it was the same me! As such, this position ended after a short time.

Initially, I had to be driven everywhere—even to work. I was dependent upon others for rides. However, I knew I could drive, and I secretly practiced during the right times (while appropriately medicated). One day, spontaneously, I packed a bag and drove four hours to my father's house for a visit. I had just my walker and a full tank of gas in tow. I was determined, and I was also becoming more and more comfortable with my walker. I had chosen to make the trip as a demonstration of my independence during my third year of recovery. Seeing my father's face as he stood in his driveway while I pulled up, sitting in the driver's seat of my car, was priceless! He walked up to me and confusedly asked me how I had driven to his house. I told him that I sat down, pushed on the gas, and steered straight to his home. We were both laughing! All who learned of this trip later were not surprised—not only that I had taken the time to practice driving secretly—but that I had made such a trip without telling anybody. Some aspects of one's personality don't change. I call it determination.

Unfortunately, shortly thereafter, while attempting to work at my private practice, I fell down another flight of stairs. I broke two ribs, dislocated my shoulder, and received another concussion. For many months, I mentally fell back into the wheelchair routine, which was much easier and presented minimal risk of falling. After months of the slow healing process and losing what I had gained in muscle, I found myself back at the pool, strengthening up for the next fall. I almost anticipated an impending doom. It was very easy to find myself in a state of depression.

In time, I got out more. I tried to take my kids on vacations or take myself out of isolation. On a vacation to Monterey Bay, I was using my walker in a very tight and delicate store that I really should not have been inside. In my defense, the store claimed it was safe for the disabled. I remember thinking as I walked in, *There is really no place for me to grab onto if I fall.* Of course, I did fall. I took down two racks of clothes with me as I hit the ground and my head on the hard cobblestone floor. As I struggled to get up—in pain and completely embarrassed—the store employee did her best to remain professional and contain her frustration. Nonetheless, she wanted to show me the door.

However, I will never forget an older woman who had the courage and empathy to grab my arm on my way out of the store and say something to the effect, "I wish my daughter could do what you just did. She will be in a wheelchair her entire life, and she will never know what it feels like to get up or to try to walk." With tears in her eyes, she smiled and walked away, validating my fall and rise. I can't explain what that meant to me. With her shared sorrow, she provided me with a positive purpose. I immediately thought of God, my children and my mother. I thought of all of the doctors and specialists who had been wrong about me. I thought of all of the people who had helped me and were counting on me. I thought of the woman's daughter who would never be able to see the store I had just fallen in. I was reenergized once again! I had a goal, a reason, a purpose! And sharing my pain with another kindred spirit made my pain seem less severe.

Approximately three years or so post-recovery, I was trying to walk about 200 yards at a beautiful beach with my walker. It seemed that, every ten yards or so, I fell backward and had to struggle back up to stand (or someone came and offered to help me). It took me two hours to walk each way in that tortuous sand. I was completely covered in sand and was called "Sand Man" by my children due to my appearance. But despite the sweat, hard work, and falls, I thought this was great exercise and progress. Despite being well beyond the one-year mark, I knew, as did my family, that I was still improving and had plenty more progress ahead.

It is hard to look back and write about the years of regression and progression. When I look back and remember the consistent falling and getting up, the illnesses, the coming and going of my abilities with respect to speech, I despair. There were constant medication changes and challenges, side effects to live with and adapt to. I had rejected and pushed away my girlfriend due to my own insecurities and depression. I felt I was becoming a consistent target of social and professional disrespect.

It was around year four, post-recovery, that I had the most trouble accepting my condition. The glimmer of day had turned into night for me, and my sense of hope had become diminished again. What had happened to me? I kept asking that question. I truly believed that I should be capable of walking. I felt as though I had put in all of the hard work, but I wasn't recovering like I should. It was so easy to look back at the past. Yet, as easy as it is to continue to look at the rear view mirror—to think about the past—it is more important for trauma survivors to look forward to a front windshield, the future! During this period, I had to remind myself daily (and be reminded by others) that there had been many accomplishments and blessings in my life throughout the four years—more than enough to fill another book. To quote English author and film director Clive Barker: "Darkness always had its part to play. Without it, how would we know when we walked in the light?" Despite my fourth year being so difficult, it will always be etched in my mind.

I want to state for the record again: *It's not how many times you fall that matters. It's how many times you get back up that will define you in almost any circumstance.*

I endured and kept pushing myself. I remembered what the doctors had said, and I continued to use positive self-talk over the years. Plus, I always kept my children and my mother in the forefront of my mind. Despite my mind saying *no* at times, I continued to lift weights, swim, and pull myself out of bed and off the ground. Yes, I was even walking unaided at times!

It was during this time that I started to walk without help for short distances, which was a tremendous accomplishment. When I did fall, I was able to easily get back up unaided. It is never a lost cause, not until one gives up or God says so. I eventually did choose to keep a year-by-year notebook as I went on. Looking back, the documents from the years after my trauma are incredible to read!

Throughout the years, so much has occurred that has allowed me to grieve, heal, and grow. Know that healing doesn't happen overnight. Although I have come so far, my journey begins again and again, sometimes every day. The same is true for all who have survived a traumatic injury or event. We all have our own timeline to strengthen ourselves (for those who seek healing). This is a very personal journey for all.

In 2010–11, I attempted to contact every neurologist, research school and "famous" university I could find. I sent out brief summaries regarding my case for possible research on me or case studies—or just plain help. I improved! Am I the only patient like me? However, it was only the Army's Veteran's Administration that took any interest in my case. After many tests and consultations with the Mayo Clinic, N.I.H, Columbia, and UCSF, only deep brain stimulation was mentioned as a potential avenue for treatment. However, after further deliberation and consultation, it was ultimately rejected because the risk was greater than the reward to the team. It was even unknown whether it would work at all in a patient such as me, or cause further damage. It certainly appears to me that I've been my own and best advocate. I've taken advice from any and all who have had somewhat similar experiences. I've studied, chatted in online medical forums, written articles regarding my case offering and seeking supports. I am currently being seen by a movement disorder specialist and senior neurologist who are learning my condition as we go along. I am her first patient with such severe myoclonus.

Over the years, I've thought quite a bit about the doctors and neurologists who say to the hopeless, "This is it!" How I was brought up and even within the profession I was trained for and am still passionate about, there is a belief that anyone who wants to change can change; it is ultimately a matter of willingness and motivation. We all have free will! Hope should always be present unless one makes the choice to be hopeless. Why on Earth would a professional promote futility with the very patients he or she is supposed to encourage and "care" for? It is a known fact in the medical world that it is *never* over—not until all mortal hope is gone. Granted, situations may change, and people may have to adapt—but to say, "This is it!" and promote hopelessness is rather irresponsible. It seems that attitude is deeply and historically entrenched within the medical community, but it must be changed! Patients should be encouraged and pushed. When I coded and died, had one doctor stood back for a second and said, "Well this is it," these pages would not have been written. I would have died. I have been given a miracle, and that is encouraging. I know I came back because "This is not it!" God and I had different plans for my life!

It has now been over five years since I've been in a traumatic trance. I have daily and social reminders of my inabilities, abilities, and skills (before and after the accident). Even while watching television commercials, I witness people doing things I am unable to do. Something as simple as climbing a ladder, holding hands while strolling down the street, dancing, skating, walking a dog or standing up in various forms is beyond me. Having people belittle and name-call me due to my physical appearance or voice is constant. Hearing the words echo to the gas attendant who pumps my gas as to why she should be doing a "man's job" while I sit in my car is always out of my control. However - Perspective is everything!

Driving down the street is also a constant reminder of where I can go and park (and where I can't go, for that matter). Going to unknown places is frightening and often embarrassing. Although most places have ADA stickers posted, most are not equipped to deal with wheelchairs. I'm still not physically able to utilize my walker for long periods of time or over the obstacle courses of what others may consider a clear pathway. Yet be that as it may, I am also reminded daily how much I have accomplished since my initial trauma. I also realize how genuinely blessed I am and I'm grateful to have experienced this journey, to have truly experienced a fuller and richer life. I am looking at the world through a new lens, a new pair of glasses—despite the seemingly negative world and social view I have looking back at me at times. How many people have this opportunity? Without this adversity and trial, I would never have experienced the amazing experiences and joys that have made me a stronger man, and that took place in my new existence and man-hood. I only hope that my children are able to value the trials and tribulations that resulted from my trauma and everything associated with it. As a family, we have all gone through a lot and have made it thus far together with love and more love. Again - Perspective is everything!

I think back to some thirty years ago, when I enlisted in the army. The slogan was, "It's not just a job, it's an adventure." Well I believe living through any form of trauma or disability is a daily adventure. For me, this book acts as a record of my traumatic brain injury resulting in action myoclonus. It's the beginning story of my journey, of how I recovered (despite my dramatic symptomology and dismal initial diagnosis). I can now say that recovery is not just a job, it's a life. Life is all about attitude. Did I mention - Perspective is everything!

Chapter 9: Grief: A Normal and Priceless Process!

I'm still grieving! Grief is a process; a lifelong process that I have written about within the chapters of this book.

Grief is generally known or referred to by the majority of people I meet as a form of deep distress, suffering, or depression.

It can also be defined more clinically as I learned in college and over the years as a person's possible behavioral response to a loss or separation. It can be real or impaired, actual or symbolic to any emotionally significant person, object or situation - which is perceived by that person to be irreconcilable or permanent I believe.

However it is defined, I believe grief is your rite of passage through trauma! I believe grief is a necessary, normal, and mandatory emotion that we all have.

It may even serve as a stepping stone toward healing if treated well. If not acknowledged or treated well, it can turn into a deeper form of grief or major depression. That depression can cause one to feel stuck within life.

Without immediate clinical support, such a condition can be fatal.

An old tale I once heard about grief dealt with a young Native American mother. She had been traumatized by the death of her infant son. Despite his death, she carried him on her back for many days afterward with the desperate hope that his life would be restored miraculously. The village felt empathy for this woman's grief, and in a short time, the people told her to seek advice from an old medicine man not far from the village. She went there immediately with the hope of getting life back for her son. Instead, however she was told by the medicine man to go back to her village and knock on every door and ask for a mustard seed from every person who had grieved or lost a loved one. She was given a glass tube to contain the seeds ... and off she went. She knocked on every door that night and throughout the next day, and to her surprise, every home had something to give her. They too had experienced grief and loss. Soon her container was overflowing with mustard seeds, and she quickly realized that every home—every person within her village—had experienced some form of grief or loss. This knowledge made her own grieving easier and allowed her to finally put her child to rest. The moral of this tale is that <u>everyone has grieved in his or her unique way.</u>

Let me say that grief is an amazing force and a *normal universal emotion* that we all have. I believe we should use it—otherwise it will abuse us! I know this to be true!

Over the course of this book, one may see how I have let myself be abused by it. I have been so grief stricken that I felt powerless and hopeless—there was no light at all. I've felt like I couldn't move. There have been days that have whisked by, and before I knew it, a week had gone by, a month had gone by. During certain periods within my journey, I often asked myself, *"Where did all the time go"*?

Grief likes nothing more than to eat our mind away like disease does to our body. Before we know it, we may not know who we are! I remember staring intently into a mirror and convinced myself that the face that stared back at me wasn't mine. I could not find or recognize the sparkle I once had. It had dimmed, and the glimmer of day had turned into night. My hope had become hopelessness at times.

Grief is not in the clinical handbook of mental illness, but it's a natural emotion that necessarily follows any traumatic event. As such, grief deserves much attention and great respect (just like any other powerful emotion). Grief is a universal experience. Honor and respect your grief!

Grief and grieving are different. I believe one can be in the process of grief for life without grieving daily. In my journey, I became familiar with many grief books and what authors had to say about depression, grief, and mourning. I had much previous experience dealing with grief in my life, but nothing could prepare me for the emotional, psychological, and physical pain I experienced as a result of the grief that occurred after my trauma on June 8, 2006!

It's indescribable, the grief I felt. There was no pill that appeared to help me from the thirty-three pills I once took daily that were prescribed for my condition.

I saw counselor after counselor, and they evaluated me for depression both in and out of the hospital. While in the third hospital, I was asked daily if I felt like hurting myself. My answer was always the same, "No, I have kids. But what would you do in my condition?" It seemed normal for me to feel depressed, yet everyone was overly anxious to treat any form of stated grief with a pill.

There was one intern I remember seeing in an out-patient setting years later (I believe in 2010). She asked me to use a scale from one to five (five meant feeling good and one meant feeling low) to answer her questions regarding depression. Upon completion of the test, she indicated that I had minimal signs of depression. This occurred on one of the worst days I remember having. She scheduled no follow-up appointment to see me despite the fact that I asked for one. I was in grief and shock the whole week prior to the appointment—and in a deeper form of grief and depression for months after that appointment.

In looking closer at grief, I remember the work of so many therapists connected with the subject. In the many workshops and seminars I attended (and the books I read) concerning this subject, I noticed a consensus regarding some universal or basic stages and forms of grief. I will address the stages I've come to learn and know: _shock, denial, anger, bargaining, depression, acceptance, and growth._

I believe it is wise to look closer at these stages because those who experience a traumatic event I believe may go through them. They may even be used as a general guideline as one transitions through the grief process.

This is simply an outline, and the stages may progress (or not) in a different order. In fact, one may fluctuate back and forth between certain stages. However, the goal (as I see it) is to get to a place where one has "grown" from his or her experience. What follows is a basic outline addressing the meaning behind the stages of shock, denial, anger, bargaining, depression, acceptance, and growth (from my perspective).

Phase	Examples...
1. Shock	"What happened to me?"
2. Denial	"I cannot believe this. Did this really happen to me?"
3. Anger	"I'm so mad this happened to me!"
4. Bargain	"If only I would have done that, this would not have happened."
5. Depression	"I'm the only one this has ever happened to."
6. Acceptance	"I accept what has happened, and I am okay now."
7. Growth	"I am a better person now."

During the initial shock and denial phases, reality has not quite sunk in. My first reaction upon hearing the bad news was one of classic shock. I had no reaction at all to the news. I blinked, nodded, and seemingly accepted the news without appearing to be troubled by it. Inside, I didn't believe it at all. I just adapted and endured. Looking back,

I foolishly believed my many months of my hospitals stays were just "quick stops". I always planned for my return to a normal life. However, initially, I had to block out all the confusing and bad news because I could not really absorb it or comprehend it fully. For the doctors to get the news through, they had to tell me countless times. A clinical psychologist was assigned to me at the last hospital. She frequently initiated conversations with me and asked whether I felt like harming myself. I know that was her job, but as I said to her over and over, "Would you?"

Grief, I believe, is the raw feeling at the center of a unique process that engages a person in adjusting to changed circumstances. Saying grief is a unique process is an understatement I realize. The power I've learned is in how we use it. We use both our mind and time. I believe grief moves a person toward adjustment. It is with hope that the adjustment is toward healing and growth.

I know that upon the long and winding road trauma survivor's travel, the stumbling blocks are huge. However, there are no problems or challenges that you will encounter without a solution! Let me say that again: There are no problems you will encounter without a solution! Finding the solution may be difficult, but let me assure you, there will always be one. As I travel my journey (and I am still accepting my ever-changing body and world), I've learned the importance of moving beyond acceptance and toward growth. Today, I am a better man than ever before! I've been through the valley of darkness, and I fear nothing! My grief, trials, tribulations, and ability to feel on every level have only strengthened me. Because of my grief, acceptance and path toward true healing, I know there is a reason for everything. What happened to me? Does it really matter?

It's not to say that every June isn't hard. It's not that looking at old photos of the old me is now easy to do. I do indeed still cry. However, I cry with strength and awareness of how far I've come, and I have within my core what all trauma survivors need in the plight of grief: Hope!

Hope. What is it? I always had the hopeful thought I was going home. Well I finally did, and it was not quite as simple as stated! What an emotional breakdown I experienced. It felt like going from one planet to another to another. However, when I landed on my new planet and explored it for a few years, there wasn't a day I allowed my internal light to fully extinguish. At times, it shined bright as a star. I had the constant loving background noise of my kids and a father role to live up to—and most importantly, I desperately wanted to! I had something to live for. My kids were my hope and future. I never stopped thinking I could do things for them, even when I couldn't. Also, I will never stop dreaming that I will be able to walk each of my daughters down the aisle as they marry (if they choose to do so).

Without hope there can be detrimental responses to grief. I used to be asked by my friends during my work as a therapist how I could tell whether someone had a clinical concern or how I could diagnose a particular client or issue. These are very difficult questions to answer with so little information. I will say that, if a symptom or concern exists for longer than reasonably expected, then it may be an issue. How do I define an issue? My answer is that

I would use how a "normal", emotionally healthy person copes and adjusts in a similar situation as a guideline. How to define a "normal" person, however, is a different book—but I hope you understand the point.

Some behaviors that may be detrimental to the management of grief have been mentioned. I've included a list of red flags here, but they are not always useful (and they certainly don't make up all the red flags one might encounter). There is no order to this list in terms of importance.

1. No display of emotion. *Remember that grief and sadness are natural emotions and your right!*

2. Going back to work immediately. *Grief takes work too ... a lot of work!*

3. Psychosomatic conditions. *Some feel like there is always something wrong!*

4. Personality changes. *The closest to him or her (or the children) are the best judges!*

5. Hostility toward unrelated objects. *This hostility can be directed at people or organizations, for example.*

6. Retreating from social activities. *This behavior is marked by isolation, changing norms, and the avoidance of contact.*

7. Detrimental/Self-Harm activities. *Sadly, there are too many to list.*

As for me, I used my grief to heal. My sadness became my goals; my goals became my hopes. I grieved and processed, and my life started to become real. I began walking with my walker down my driveway, down the street, and then around the block until I worked up to 1 mile per day (and then 2 miles per day … and then even more). Most importantly, after all those doctors said I would never walk again, talk again, or be independent, I proved them wrong. This is *not* it!

Remember: grief is powerful and normal. A trauma survivor will certainly grieve from time to time, but that grief can also serve as a reminder of new goals and how far the person has come! Use your grief (and the process) positively for the only way to get through grief is to go straight through it!

Chapter 10: Healing in Time!

Healing is timeless, and I continue to heal and grow daily. Like grief, I believe healing is a lifelong process. I'm still healing and growing and will forever do so. People can tell you how you *may* heal, but no one can tell you when you *will* heal! I believe that only you can make that decision … with support!

True healing is extremely difficult for a trauma survivor. Experiencing pain and crying are easy, but overcoming that thorny hill of grief and moving toward healing takes incredible work. Healing is another process that one must endure following a trauma. Another hill! However, this phase is the top of the mountain. I see Grief as the sides of the mountain. After all the blood, sweat, and tears, one becomes comfortable with his or her place in life. However, if that internal wound is not treated, it may become infected and cause discomfort in life. The person may not heal and find himself or herself back on the slippery slope of the side of that mountain of life … forever!

For example, if you have a wound (such as a cut on your arm) and do nothing to treat it, it may become infected and painful—and it may leave a scar. However, if you treat that very same wound with a cleaning solution and take proper care of the area, it may become less painful. Over time, it will heal and (possibly) go unnoticed for the rest of your life. The same applies here!

Healing for me is about trauma survivors being able to clean those specific areas by making positive changes in their daily life. Specifically, healing means changing major life patterns. For me such changes required shifting my way of thinking! This can be a very challenging task, but it can be done. *Stinky thinking* is what I call the distortion of our thoughts and making our reality worse than it really is. I engaged in this sort of thinking quite often (as I think is true for many trauma survivors). This prevents healing.

I believed for a long time that every person was against me due to my disability. In fact, there have been so many who sacrificed and offered time and service to assist me. This selfishness on my part only took away my sense of hope and healing.

Even if you have a setback (as we all do), you must realize that it's part of the healing process. If you have taken four steps forward in treatment and go back one step, you're still three steps ahead from where you started! I've always wondered how there could be triumphs without any trials. Once a positive lifestyle becomes a part of your daily routine, it is easier to keep going and head toward healing. But life is constantly changing, and your routine can sometimes get thrown off. Maybe you've had a bad day, and you just couldn't find the time to do your usual routine. That in itself has thrown me off for days. But healing is getting beyond those days. I know that once your structure and balance are thrown off, it is easy to find excuses or reasons not to start back up again.

One must constantly strive to move forward in the healing process. This is not to say that you always will each and every day, but one must have the motivation to continue to do so. From my own experience, it is too easy to slip into old habits. I suggest placing positive and visible affirmations throughout your home. Wherever you go within your home, you should see signs of your goals, hopes, or improvements. I have done this by myself and with others, and I've seen incredibly positive effects. What you see can lift your spirits to the sky. This is, in part, what is needed to improve your lifestyle and create even more hope. That new lifestyle is a cornerstone of healing.

In the process of healing, always try to remember what you've already accomplished. Change is not easy, but it is a certainty. It will happen regardless of your wishes. Why not be in charge of those changes with hope rather than being helpless? Always remember that you are a survivor (not a victim), and you must maintain that mindset! Believe me: making thoughtful and meaningful changes in your life following a traumatic event is critical and not easy. However, it's important not to let someone else dictate your life—that may prove to be disempowering and prevent true healing and growth.

As stated earlier, no one thinks he or she will become a trauma survivor. However, if you do … you do! Though that rear-view mirror might sneak up on you (and it will), you must create a new persona in order to heal. You are the same you, but you have adapted. And most importantly, you now have a positive perspective and hope! You are in charge of how to heal (along with your support team). You are in the driver's seat and looking forward toward that great big windshield. You know where to steer your life. I believe no one else will know what will work best for you … and that insight will come in time.

With healing, there needs to be support. Support comes in many forms, but love and care from your family and loved ones are most important. Other support may include involvement with counseling, in-home health support services, occupational therapy, physical therapy, speech therapy, county local programs, life alert, etc…

When you are able to (and feel like you can) move forward, you can work with your support person or team to make a plan. The plan should include what you've learned from your "days off," and it should remind you what's available to you. If you aren't ready and find yourself still grieving, give yourself time with your support. It's okay! One step at a time! Keep reminding yourself of the positive things that may come or may have already come from the changes you've made thus far. These changes may be very simple: less stiffness in your movements, easier transitions, more comfortable breathing, greater emotional strength, etc. I believe one can always find something as good or better today than what one found the previous day—no matter what.

Each day the sun rises is a new day, and it's the best day to begin the changes that could make a difference in how you think, feel, and act! Remember, no matter how many clouds are above your head, the sun still shines! As Allan Watts says, "The only way to make sense out of change is to plunge into it, move with it, and join the dance."

Treat every day as a special event. I don't mean just opening your eyes or getting out of bed—I mean being mindful of the new day. As a trauma survivor, this is important in the healing process. I read somewhere that being positive and ambitious is the number one factor that contributes to healing and creating a better life. Focus on what is important to you, and place your attention, intention, energy, and hope there—healing may come. This make's sense to me!

I suggest changing something every week. Choose what you will do differently well beforehand. Commit to making these changes. What happens when you commit yourself and keep to that commitment is that you trust yourself more I believe. We are very good at giving our word to authorities, our doctors, our families, and our friends, but what about ourselves? Do we keep promises to ourselves? I do not believe we do much of the time. If we are to heal, we must focus on our commitment to ourselves and rid ourselves of that stinky thinking! No matter how small your commitments or goals, the faithfulness to yourself creates a reminder and builds upon your own character, well-being, and healing!

There is no question that all trauma survivors should honor their body and mind to heal. Respect that! No matter how much strife we face, we must pay attention to our bodies and minds. A key to healing is to be proactive and support our own mental, emotional, and physical selves!

I suggest beginning slowly and working toward a more optimal way of living. A few simple reminders from several individuals took a long time to sink in for me. They suggested that I get rest. If your body continues to run on empty, you will eventually run out of gas.

Diet is essential. You are what you eat. To heal, you must eat in a healthful manner. I am not a nutritionist, but I do remember now to drink protein shakes daily and am careful in choosing wholesome foods for my meals.

If you're able, move your body in any way that makes you happy! Whether you are in a bed or able to use a treadmill, some form of regular activity will be a definite boost to your overall healing.

In the effort to heal, there must be time created to treat yourself well. A lesson I was taught early in life was that the greatest gift we can give ourselves and our loved ones is a well-lived life.

I also strongly recommend therapeutic counseling following a trauma event. It can assist one in the healing process incredibly. I have found in my previous career that there are many misconceptions about counseling. I suggest that someone in a state of grief or depression should see a licensed specialist who <u>specifically deals with that area</u>. Just because someone has fancy letters by his or her name within the profession, it does not mean he or she has the experience to deal with a trauma survivor. Just like you would check out several different places before buying a new car, I suggest calling several places, agencies, therapist's and asking whether they have specialists in the desired area.

These suggestions have helped me and provided tremendous value in my life in terms of healing, growth and maintaining hope! They can only help trauma survivors. My personal hope is that you will become content and eventually heal throughout your own incredible journey. Isn't that what this is all about?

Chapter 11: Fifteen Tips for Trauma Survivors and Their Loved Ones!

In terms of caring for a trauma patient, I believe I am going against the major medical establishment by saying there is nothing better for a trauma survivor's healing than <u>love!</u> There is just no doctor or pill that can compare. I've had my share of care providers, therapists, medications, treatments and hospital stays, but I believe loved ones and families are the roots that allow healing, growth, and success to take place.

I have provided some simple suggestions for the trauma survivor, family member, or friend once the survivor is home.

Each survivor is different! Some will require activity and a physician's or care provider's approval or assistance, and some will not.

Our friends and support network have their own lives and often get busy, and this sometimes means we get forgotten! We need our peer groups—our friends, our loved ones—to show that they "care" and remember us. After all, we're still alive!

TIP 1

Love your friend

- This may require nothing more than thoughts and prayers. There is great power in these practices.

- The question is how will he or she know about your love?

- Show your love and compassion in your own unique way. Ensure your loved one knows that he or she has not been forgotten by you! Love your friend not just in the hospital or the day he or she returns home—express yourself as long as you are a "friend."

TIP 2

Be there for your friend after he or she returns home

- Round up visitors and be there! This does not mean a phone call—friends, people should be there in support.

- People do appreciate cards and notes, but a visit is better. A visit will create a lasting memory, but a card will usually be put in a stack or thrown away after a while.

- Make mental notes about what you plan to do. Even with the best of intentions people tend to be there in the beginning more than the end! Realistically look at your schedule and set a time to be there.

TIP 3

If you live far away, find a way to connect to your loved one

- In this era of technology (in which everyone wants to save time and have all the latest gadgets), isn't it strange that people seem more concerned about a few roaming minutes on their cell phone than their friends? Some people seem too busy for a five minute chat and check in with someone who went through a battle for his or her life?

- Call. When you can, let your friend hear your voice. The love and concern in your voice are very important.

- If he or she is able to interface with you on the computer so that you feel that much closer -- Make it happen!

- There could be a regular routine set up initially that is convenient for both of you. Believe me, that contact may be all the trauma survivor has to look forward to all day or week, and when it comes, it is glorious! When it is forgotten, it is heartbreaking!

TIP 4

Attempt to understand his or her trauma!

- This requires huge effort and empathy! Also, be willing to embrace the pain of your loved one's trauma and suffering. It is easier to avoid, deny, or minimize it, but those strategies prevent your friend from sharing his or her life and strengthening his or her friendship with you.

- Your loved one has already gone "insane" before your attempts to understand. However, in your attempts to understand his or her trauma, please be patient. Do not be afraid to inquire directly. Talking about his or her experience within the safety of a loved one's presence is comforting—despite the tears that may come and go. Crying is okay! Expression will allow for greater understanding.

- Realize that there will be days of depression. Your goal is to be a friend in those moments.

TIP 5

Don't be afraid to talk about pre-trauma memories

- When someone goes through a trauma, part of that person lives on through memory, past friendships, and days of glory.

- Your friend is not afraid to actively remember the person who existed before the trauma. Positively communicate those memories to him or her. It is empowering and may make the trauma survivor believe that he or she can do it again! That is not a bad thing...."hope"!

- Remembering the past sometimes makes hoping for the future possible.

Tip 6

Don't be afraid of discussing post-trauma hopes and plans together

- Developing a new identity is needed because the way people and society will define him or her will significantly change over time. Open, honest and hopeful communication is needed.

- It is arduous work to reconstruct oneself; "it takes more than a family, it takes a community of hope."

- Keep setting and if needed, erasing hopes and goals. Never discuss giving up.

TIP 7

What to say

- Say the following: I've been thinking about you. You're on my mind. I love you. I missed you. I want to help you. I can help you. I will help you. I'll check in on you weekly. You can get through this. You've survived this!

- But always say what you mean and mean what you say!

TIP 8

Allow your friend to cry and cry with your friend

- Crying and tears are a natural and pure way to grieve and heal. It's okay (and quite natural) to cry! In fact, it's good to cry when needed, and one may feel a sense of release when crying. Tears are a form of mourning, and I believe they are sacred.

- Many feel uncomfortable crying in front of others. For the love of your friend, do not be one of those people.

- Should your friend begin to cry, be a friend! This may make your friendship only stronger.

TIP 9

Reach out to your friend with hugs, touch, and love

- Physical and loving contact is healing! Don't be afraid to touch and hug!

- Have you hugged your traumatized friend ever? Have you held his or her hand or put your arm around him or her? If not, now is the time to do so!

- Hugging is an ancient tradition, and it will be more memorable than words for many.

TIP 10

Cook or clean for your friend

- Meals are sometimes forgotten. Cooking or mealtime can be extremely difficult for a trauma survivor. Loved ones and friends should rotate when available and play chef!

- Plan an evening when you can cook a meal for him or her or the entire family—and have a fun and relaxing evening. For the trauma survivor, it is like having a restaurant come to him or her—but it's better, because he or she is dining with loved ones!

- Additionally, cleaning is something we don't think about much (or even do for ourselves often). Trauma survivors become more aware of what they can't do, and for me, cleaning was always on my mind. Create a plan with friends and family to help with chores that will bring an endless smile to the face of your loved one. While there, you may also be able to accomplish many of the other tips suggested in this book.

- If you can't be present, possibly purchase a gift certificate to a larger chain cleaning service that is bonded for regularly scheduled cleanings. Pair up with a friend to share the expense for an extended amount of time. This will provide well-needed support for the trauma survivor and allow more free time for the family and other caregivers.

TIP 11

<u>Get out!</u>

- If possible, get out and see the world! A change of view may offer a well-deserved break from the focus on their needs and tasks. Plan excursions to fit the conditions/needs of the survivor. Seek to create an environment of tranquility and peace!

- Invite your friend to your home for a meal. This should be a normal action with or without trauma. Invite your friend anywhere that is realistic for him or her.

- If you are a person of faith, invite your friend to a special activity at your place of worship. This will offer a platform for positive interaction and conversation.

- Attend a play or concert. Check online for ADA seating or simply request special seating at the time of ticket purchase.

TIP 12

The new bucket list

- Create a "bucket list" with your friend, and then modify it so he or she is capable of achieving some of his or her wishes and goals. This keeps ones mind moving forward.

- This is huge and cannot be over stated!!

TIP 13

Play ball!

- If the trauma survivor is a sports enthusiast, plan to attend a sporting event. National organized sports activities offer many specialized ADA accommodations.

- Local high schools, colleges and universities provide a wealth of sporting (and other) venues that are also ADA accessible. The variety of sports and activities may be inspiring to the survivor and help him or her set new personal goals.

TIP 14

Keep it realistic

- Relationships in general are hard and full of compromise. A good relationship involves equal compromise and work from the people in it.

The fact is -- a trauma survivor with a disability doesn't contribute less to a relationship! He or she may do less of the heavy lifting, but how important is that in a relationship? Share yourself; enjoy the other as a person! Enjoy life with your friend! Also, if you live long enough, you will probably enter into a relationship with someone with a disability or have one yourself. Treat people how you would want to be treated. Compassion, kindness and love are the key.

Tip 15

- **Create your own tip(s) for you and your loved one**

_____

_____

_____

_____

_____

Chapter 12: Conclusion -

Now, as I go into my sixth year post-trauma (and the sixth year of my recovery), I note that there has been much said and yet, so much left unsaid. I find myself wondering how there can be any kind of conclusion to this book when there will never be an end to my life's journey. I will never give up this fight or stop working toward improving the quality of my life.

I don't often regret my new path. I have worked too hard for the opposite to have regrets. I want to share my experiences, my strengths, my passions, and (especially) my hopes with my children and other survivors of trauma in a positive and unforgettable way!

However, I am reminded that, when there is one trauma survivor, there are many others helplessly involved as well. The past years have shown me the powerlessness of other survivors. My own family members and loved ones have minimal to no support of their own. This journey has shown me the tremendous weight and burden—the shame and guilt—that these supporters must grapple with.

The average person averts his or her eyes and is not instantly capable of accepting or knowing how to deal with trauma or the pain in others. There will be awkwardness for all involved— even for all of my own roots. Pay particular attention not only to the survivor on center stage, but also to his or her children. Children mostly do not avert their eyes, and they may feel especially afraid and need extra and appropriate developmental attention and support.

Throughout this book, I have tried to offer many different insights into the world of trauma survivors. I'm reminded that my initial intent was to offer determination and hope to those who need it. I sought to help others discover their own journey by sharing the steps I took on my own journey.

My other hope was to inspire the reader to document his or her own journey in the face of trauma, shock, and grief.

I was determined to offer some insight of the before, during, and after of my own particular trauma—to tell my own story. Though my condition is unique medically, many of my experiences are very similar to those of other trauma survivors. It was my negative experiences in a hospital that eventually made me want to generate interest in the lack of care so many receive. I feel a strong need to put the meaning of "*care*" back into that word and to advocate for those who can't speak for themselves! Not all hospital staff should be instantly trusted. If you have doubts, listen to your instincts. My advice to friends and family again is to be there as often as possible—and even drop by unannounced if you can.

The hospital system also focuses on getting patients in and out as quickly as they can. They will try to release you or your loved one as soon as possible, leaving the patient responsible for finding long-term rehabilitation and support. It's my opinion that you should try every avenue. You may not achieve your old life, but you will achieve a better life should you try.

During my journey in writing this book, I found it necessary to share the true hopelessness and grief that I experienced as a trauma survivor and disabled man returning home. For the afflicted, newly disabled, or trauma survivor, it's a moment-to-moment, hour-to-hour, day-to-day process of living fully despite the challenges. It's learning to remain graceful, grateful, and spiritually connected. It's trying to be consciously aware and doing and learning things you didn't have to do before. For family and friends, it may be gaining a better understanding of the challenges faced, learning how to truly be supportive, and learning how to listen to the expert: the survivor!

It is important to remember that both groups are essentially in uncharted waters. If this book helps you to sail down your own path, your own journey, then it will have been a success in my opinion. Never lose sight of the truth: you have a right to heal, sail, and move forward—no matter what the circumstances!

If one is able to begin that internal, soul-nourishing work—not only for a sense of validation, but also to help along the grieving and healing process—one will be better off. Take those positive steps toward healing emotionally, medically, mentally, psychologically, physically, socially, and spiritually. Know that there is a life ahead of you—it's up to you to endure it or enjoy it. I say enjoy it!

All survivors should understand that they are indeed miracles! They are *survivors!* Stay positive in regards to your valued existence. You are the Giant Oak Tree, and you have roots! You are loved by family and friends, and you are one of God's children. Try not to isolate yourself. Try to remember to stay grateful! Stay straight in the middle of your road of life after you survive your trauma.

Finally, this is *never* it! After all, we have redefined what normal is. *I believe that if you can survive a trauma, you can survive the aftermath!* Remember: this is not it until God says it is. <u>Seize your day!</u>

In closing…..

I Believe …

That maturity has more to do with what
types of experiences you've had and what
you've learned from them and less to do with
how many birthdays you've celebrated.

I Believe …

That our background and circumstances
may have influenced who we are, but
we are responsible for who we become.

I Believe …

That we are responsible for our actions—
no matter how we may feel at times.

I Believe …

That either you control your attitude
or it will control you!

I Believe …

That we don't have to change friends if
we understand that friends will change.

I Believe …

That sometimes the people you expect
to kick you when you're down
will be the ones to help you get back up.

I Believe …

That even when you think you have no
more to give, when a friend needs you,
you will find the strength to help.

I Believe …

That your life can be changed in a matter of
seconds, minutes, hours by people
who don't even know you.

I Believe …

That you can keep going long after you think you can't.

I Believe …

That hero's are the people who do what
has to be done when it needs
to be done—regardless of the consequences.

I Believe …

That it isn't always enough to be forgiven by others.
Sometimes you have to learn to forgive yourself.

I Believe …

That no matter how bad your heart is broken,
the world doesn't stop for your grief.

I Believe …

That the happiest of people don't necessarily
have the best of everything—
they just make the most of everything they have.

I Believe …

That it's taking me a long time and continues to be an
ongoing process to become the person I want to be.

I Believe …

That you should always leave loved ones with
loving words. It may be the last time you see them.

I Believe …

That the people you care about most in life
can be taken from you too soon.

I Believe … in you!

*Please believe in yourself, treasure your
experiences and make the most of your life!*

This is Not it!

Author Autobiography

Brett Green, M.A., L.M.F.T. (Licensed Marriage & Family Therapist), has tremendous expertise and experience in regards to the personal journey of trauma survivors. He seeks to help those in need find their unique paths in the worlds of grief, healing, growth, recovery.

He has been in the mental health field for nearly twenty-two years. His career is truly eclectic in that he started as a probation counselor before transitioning into a part-time county mental health position where he felt he could do more and serve more children, individuals and families.

He later became the coordinator of a nonprofit agency overseeing an adult outpatient program that provided established, interesting, quality and unique services to an excess of 350 clients per week.

His administrative abilities and clinical insight eventually found him working as a family court mediator in two separate counties and court systems. He was tasked with mediating between disputing high-conflict parents in both superior courts, while making child custody recommendations that always maintained the best interests of the children in mind.

During this phase, he also opened up a private practice office and earned county certifications to operate a child abuse and neglect program and a domestic violence education program. This practice has grown and offers six separate programs. He also serves the individual or family needing one-on-one therapeutic supports as well.

However, in 2006, at the apex of his career, he experienced a traumatic brain injury that forever changed his life. Although his private practice remained in operation, his focus is now on advocating for trauma survivors and the disabled—people misunderstood, unrepresented and (quite often) still neglected!

He now offers a very unique and experienced blend of therapeutic services, workshops, and presentations. These services include advocacy for trauma survivors and disabled people. He also provides expertise and insight in the following arenas: the management of anger, child abuse prevention, domestic violence intervention, family enrichment and positive parenting education, and high-conflict parenting and private mediation counseling. He has been a "court appointed expert" in both child custody and domestic violence cases. He is an expert in movement disorders, action myoclonus specifically.

His goal is not to provide information to the public merely. He seeks to educate and change lives within each counseling session or workshop presentation so the participant leaves with a new perspective.

He was most recently selected to be a member of the California State Department of Mental Health - Human Resources (NP) committee. He hopes to work specifically to advance the underrepresented culture of disabled people (including trauma survivors).

He sincerely hopes that people will find a renewed strength after reading the experiences detailed within this book. He hopes they can begin to regain their own sense of normalcy and right to grieve! This may ultimately serve as a stepping stone toward true healing. As stated, he believes we all have the right to move forward and heal—no matter what the circumstances are! It's not how many times we fall that will define us… it's how many times we choose to get back up that will!